Little Money
BIG
CREDIT

How The Wealthy Got There

K. BOTWE

LIST OF CONTENT

Introduction 7

Section I: Think And Speak Asset

Chapter One: Learn to Earn the Wealthy Way 14

Chapter Two: Establish & Maintain Great Credit 51

Chapter Three: Save Short Term Money for Assets 87

Section II: A Million Dollar Line

Chapter Four: Build Business Systems of Success 113

Chapter Five: Create Processes for Multiple Streams 128

Section III: Transgenerational Wealth & Giving Back

Chapter Six: Diversify Asset Classes Using More Debt 150

Chapter Seven: Asset Protection 160

Conclusion 173

All rights reserved. No part of this book may be reproduced or transmitted in any form without permission in writing from the author. For information, contact:

Kenko Publishing Corporation

8245 Mills Rd

Houston Texas 77064

281-901-0158

www.DeviseWealth.com

Email: Info@DeviseWealth.com

DeviseWealth@gmail.com

Facebook Group: *DeviseWealthMastermind*

Twitter: *@KennethBotwe*

YouTube: *KennethBotwe*

LinkedIn: *Ken Botwe*

Facebook: *Ken Botwe*

Instagram: *KenBotwe*

Pinterest: *KenBotwe*

This book is intended to be used as a reference and readers must do their own independent verification. The author or the publisher is not rendering any legal, financial, tax or business advice and disclaim any personal liability from the content within. Care was used in the preparation of this document however, the author and publisher assume no responsibility for any errors herein.

Other Publications & Educational Materials by the Author

Facebook Group: *DeviseWealthMastermind*

Join and get FREE Webinar: Inspire to Make You Money

Join and get FREE e-Course: Debt Elimination – How to Get Out of Debt

E-book: *5 Principles for Becoming Wealthy*

Buy at <u>Amazon.com</u> or download FREE at <u>DeviseWealth.com</u>

Find The Publications Below at DeviseWealth.com

e-Courses:

Debt Elimination

Pay Off Your House in 5 Years

Establish Great Credit

Save Short-term Money for Assets

How to Build Wealth Forever

Much more...

Blog:

5 Reasons why many People are not Rich

Steps for Great Credit

Becoming Wealthy from The bottom up

Bitcoins and ICO's

Much more...

New Videos Every Week at YouTube.com/user/KennethBotwe

5 Mindset for Success Series

First thing you must do to Become Wealthy

How to get out of Debt

5 Benefits of Having a Credit Card

Payoff your House in 5 Years

Much more...

Dedication

In loving memories of Isaac, Elvenor and Berlese Botwe. To my family and friends, thank you for the continued inspiration. My gratitude to my team, for you are forever appreciated.

To my current and future students, I promise to stay relentless in my quest to help you transform your life and become financially FREE through education.

Introduction

Substantial wealth can be accumulated through a variety of systems. Notice I said variety because the focus is to build wealth but the means to get there varies. Like mathematics, there are several methods that can be used to solve a challenge however there is only one correct answer. In this case, the correct answer is devising wealth for yourself with sub benefits reaching your family, friends, community, and the world as a whole. The genesis of it may be slow but if the systems are executed correctly, it accelerates within a few years.

Depending on your current situation and access to resources, you could start accumulating wealth in hundreds, thousands, millions or tens of millions and beyond. Then once the mechanism is in motion, the growth becomes bigger as time progresses. The key word I want you to get very familiar with is "Assets". In its simplest form, it makes you money. How often and for how long are questions that can scientifically be answered once the type of asset has been identified and examined.

Going forward, you must think and speak asset. In other words, it should be on your mind and in your vocabulary. Before we dive in, let me admit, I have not always been privy to the systems of becoming wealthy. I've however consistently tried to find my way and made many mistakes along the way. From failed ventures to solo initiatives, something seemed to be missing. I read a lot of books, attended many seminars, and talked to a multitude of successful people internationally,

nationally and locally. Clarity was not attained because almost everyone had a unique style that worked for them. Success was all around me, but the clues were not all there, so designing one for myself posed a bit of a challenge.

It wasn't until the year 2006, during a deep meditation one evening while alone that a recollection of my very first business as a preteen began to circulate through my mind. It was useless trying to shake this memory as it played over and over again. Suddenly, it dawned on me. My ideas were not fully developed and it lacked essential systems, yet I continued to operate the same way. I believe it was Albert Einstein, who is credited with the saying not to do the same thing over again expecting a dissimilar result. The moment of truth had arrived. To clear my head and try a different approach, I went on a vacation to South Padre Island from Houston with a few family friends on our motorcycles. Upon our return, my new idea began to take shape.

Many lessons have been learned, observed and documented. Among these lessons, there was a major key point encompassing scientific systems and processes to create wealth. They include profitable businesses and investments that are properly structured. The use of little money and big credit through leverage is the most important key among the processes. From inception, the business apparatus must have built-in protection and some activated later at various levels. The creation of wealth itself must be treated like an institution. Building a talented support team that understands their roles and believes in the vision is primal. Please note that knowing how to become wealthy alone will not suffice.

Whether a new creation or existing, taking action and turning ideas into constructive and innovative strategic wealth systems that solves a common problem will get you closer. Scaling these wealth systems to serve the masses will make you cash rich. Cash, however, may or may not retain its value in the future. Convert it into more assets that increase in value over time while producing significant cash flow to reinforce your wealth. The structure must be equipped with investments that by nature takes advantage of tax incentives while using arbitrage and leverage processes to further expedite wealth.

Preserve the systems and processes of wealth as it continues to grow into trans-generational wealth and you now have the recipe for becoming rich forever for generations to come. The protection of all assets is indeed of vital importance as you'll see throughout the book. My assignment is to dissect every aspect of the systems and reveal how to properly assemble wealth. Among other major wealth systems, are processes of initial capital acquisition, systems of utilization of money, credit, debt, asset protection, sound business, investments model, and finally processes for giving back in the form of charity. Your assignment is to take action when you feel you have the correct comprehension to building your wealth.

I have committed myself to helping anyone with wealth ambitions so long as they initiate the implementation process. For that reason, I write in a simple and easy fashion so that everyone can apply these methods and strategies. There is nothing more gratifying than seeing people wining. I enjoy having the talent and ability to serve others. With discipline and planning, those that are properly conditioned and positioned will prevail.

For long, my story may have been just like yours. In spite of the fact that opportunities are abundant worldwide and especially here in the United States of America, a vast majority of people are still struggling to meet their obligation, let alone build wealth. To many, the American dream seems far fetch and unattainable, leaving them in mediocre. It seems there is nowhere to turn for answers because the so-called financial gurus talk too slick for the ordinary person to really follow.

Their programs are too expensive to purchase and there has been no simple, time friendly, or hold you by the hand book that a reader can follow to earn a substantial income, eliminate bad debt and acquire wealth. Existing publications are either incomplete, too complicated or extremely time-consuming and even outdated. If a large quantity of people in the land of opportunity feels helpless in terms of building wealth, imagine the plight of others worldwide.

As the title suggests, organic wealth is achieved through little money and big credit and most of the 33 million millionaires worldwide of the 7.5 billion worldwide population utilize this method. These people operate under concepts designed to help them win. To alleviate the hindrance we'll look a bit deeper to unmasked proven, relevant, and fresh methods for easy digestion. The methodology makes it practical for everyone that has an ambition for success, regardless of the current circumstances or geographic location. Just look at companies like Uber, Netflix, Legal Shield, Amazon, Alibaba, Facebook and Instagram to name a few. With the emergence of the internet, information technology, and financial technology such as Blockchain and cryptocurrencies like Bitcoin, the possibilities are endless.

The ability to conduct all types of business functions not previously possible without the internet is a reality. Anyone can create and market products and services without billboard, television, or radio ads. Networking has never been easier, and webinars are on full throttle all across the globe. Amazingly, all the above-mentioned functions can be done wherever you are on the globe with just your Smartphone. Now comes the latest in Fintech, so conducting exchanges on a decentralized cryptography platform is becoming an alternative that many experts in the field believe will reshape the very nature of finance, economics, commerce and maybe even politics. Combine all of these elements and it is more conducive to acquire wealth now more than ever before.

This is not a get rich quick book. There is no such thing other than maybe an inheritance, superstardom, or the enormous odds of possibly winning the lottery. The information contained in these pages are designed to educate and reveal practical ways to generate initial capital, establish great credit and leverage it for wealth. The contents range from showing how individuals with no cash can transform their status and begin to make money, how the working class employee can take smart measures to transform from an employee into an employer, and how the successful entrepreneur can reach the next level building a portfolio of asset classes and its protective apparatus.

For the beginner with no extra money at all, you will explore a multitude of ways to change your circumstance. You will be introduced to real-time action steps that will put money in your hands within days. An overabundance of ways will be revealed. Indeed, these funds should be used to start a real low cost scalable and profitable business. The systems covered here will enable you to operate with minimum staff, inventory, and consequently low overhead.

When profits begin to accumulate, you'll then propel to the next level. Soon you will reach a point where your systems will enable you to generate money around the clock even when you are asleep. When utilized, the systems will benefit anyone who desires to be build wealth. All people of influence should share this book with their community, and parents should share the knowledge gained with their teenage children and beyond.

When I began the concept for the book, I wanted to create a solution that would benefit everyone in a transformational way. One which comes not only from my own successful strategies but others I'm affiliated with and researched entities all the same.

People often ask me how and where to start in terms of acquiring wealth. The answer is not a one size fit all. Circumstances differ in terms of resources, passion, and capacity. Being fully aware of the challenges involved when writing to such broad audiences, I decided to break this book down into three sections. This methodology and style afford me the opportunity to talk directly to unique individuals with drive and determination but undeveloped ideas, unsubstantial capital, sub-par credit and no clear business plan. Various systems for achieving a strong business foundation and then building upon it are all covered.

In a systematic order, section two is geared towards graduates of section one and generally anyone who is prepared to make an investment for greater returns. This section elevates strategies to advance levels so the reader can take on bigger business aspirations all the way into the million dollar line and beyond. This section deals with determining when to expand as well as the recipe for acquiring various asset classes to accelerate the growth process.

I have dedicated section three to showing a number of diverse systems that can help to protect your accumulated wealth instead of leaving it to other financial institutions. We are talking about trans-generational wealth so that all your assets are preserved and passed down to your family. Indeed, there are key actions that must be taken to protect all your assets.

Lastly, suggestions are made on how to properly pay it forward so that any assistance you give to the less fortunate is actually used for that purpose and proves effective. I wish that you enjoy reading this book as much as I did writing it.

Section I

THINK AND SPEAK ASSET

CHAPTER ONE

Learn to Earn the Wealthy Way

Every single venture you choose to embark upon should begin with Learning and Familiarity.

Prerequisite Skills for Wealth Creation

As a good swimmer has a great chance of surviving for a period of time in open waters, someone who does not know how to swim is sure to drown under the same circumstances. The difference is the skill set. The same concept is true in terms of building wealth, though a different set of skills are required. It is the prerequisite for wealth creation. In other words, there are things that one must be proficient in if they are to become and remain rich.

Our school system, for the most part, fails to teach financial literacy skills to students and lot of parents either do not possess the financial background or have the wrong information. Others may know bits and pieces but nothing useful in a real effective way. If all things money were widely taught in schools, churches, mosque, synagogues, temples or other places of mass meetings and applied, a great transformation would occur. Humankind finances and economic prosperity would spread to a much larger population of people. The spread would benefit much more people even in less fortunate circumstances. I remain convinced that wealth to more people is inevitable since an enormous amount only belongs to the top one percent. Besides, the already wealthy would not lose their money because more would be created and the global economy as a whole will boom.

Beneficiaries of the skills would become rich and many would, in turn, create jobs and charities to assist those that do not have the ambition. The more wealthy people we have in our society, the better off our human family would be, so it's of vital importance that I do all I can to teach, knowing fully well that not all the people I reach will utilize the knowledge. I am however more than satisfied if a small group of at least ten percent of my readers benefit from it.

Skill One

The first skill that one must master is the utilization of money and how to transform it into various forms to build infinite wealth. You are considered proficient when you can use this skill to build wealth systems over and over again. In the event you lose all your money for whatever reason, you are able to rebuild in a short period of time. If faced with the same scenario, persons without these skills would crumble and fall. They would lose their entire fortune and may become broke permanently. Many would criticize such people but they themselves may not prevail unless they know how to constantly transform money. Any amount of money would eventually be diminished without knowing the proper use, therefore, it is my wish that more people learn and apply the skills of multiple income generation.

To do it, the mindset about money has to be correct. Money is a tool that must stay busy and should not be allowed to remain idle. It does not get tired as humans and animals do. It is highly fertile and works best when in constant transformation. It grows when it moves in the right direction and shrinks when misused. It is also regarded as imaginary most of the time by those that really know and understand it. There are simple processes to get lots of it but if you work too hard for it, you'll never get enough. The key is to make it work for you twenty-four hours a day and three hundred sixty-five days every single year.

Money is loyal, take care of it and it will reciprocate the love by constantly increasing. If you leave it in the bank instead of working it, the bank will gladly do it for you and give you 1 percent of the proceeds in interest. What a shame for anyone to allow the banks to reap the benefits of their money. It seems everyone likes money although many don't take the time to get to know it really well. It is very colorful but simple as an object can be. Having the wealth skills is like having a money machine so even when it changes its nature, it is irrelevant to you because you'll just print more. Most people get it by selling their time and that's fine however there are only 24 hours in a day. You have to live, sleep, eat, spend time with loved ones, and enjoy life, so that cannot be the best way to get it.

Put money to work, borrow more and put it to work. Repeat the cycle and you'll build wealth faster than working for it a whole lifetime. Imagine getting seventy-five to ninety dollars on every one hundred dollars you have. Wouldn't that be much better than going to work for the entire one hundred dollars? This imagination can be your reality as it is for me but first, you must familiarize yourself with the rules of getting that money without sacrificing all your time and labor. Yes, some work is required but it's on your terms and not some employer. Your imagination of gaining up to ninety percent on your money is a reality called credit. Hence the title Little Money Big Credit – How The Wealthy Got There.

Here are two quick examples to illustrate my point with a rental property investment. A motivated but financially illiterate person

(Person A) has one hundred thousand dollars to invest in a rental real estate with cash flow potential of five hundred dollars a month. It cost person A the entire one hundred grand to do the deal and is now receiving six thousand dollars a year from this investment after all expenses. Another motivated person with some financial education (Person B) would buy five rental properties instead. Person B would have enough concept of money and credit and so he or she would borrow eighty percent from a lender and pay twenty thousand out of pocket for each one. The result is twenty-five thousand dollars a year after all expenses. Person B is now excited and wants to learn to earn more.

This is an example of a system that is utilized by everyone that's financially astute from nations, to kingdoms, to fortune 500 companies to moguls but even the ordinary man or woman like you and I can use it as well to build wealth. With great credit, you get to borrow lots of money, then more money. If you know the requirements, you can follow it to secure more money. How would you make it grow, you might ask? Transform it into assets like a profitable business, real estate, or other investments that generate cash flow. The assets should be fixed so that it can produce cash flow on a constant basis. When you secure such an asset, never sell it outright but feel free to exchange it for a bigger asset with an increase in cash flow. The right assets will also appreciate in value over time, a noteworthy benefit. It will also benefit you in tax savings through depreciation deductions. Treat it like a racehorse, don't get rid of it unless you find a faster horse. The trajectory is now set for becoming wealthy when you have reached this level of learning and applying the lessons for successful asset acquisition.

Skill Two

The second skill is properly protecting your wealth system so it can never be taken away from you by thieves of all kinds. Some wear suits while others conceal who they are but wouldn't hesitate to take your money from you. Take the correct protective measure so you can focus on acquiring more assets not fighting to keep what you already have. Protect your wealth against litigation, theft, loss and fraud and last but not least protect it from excessive tax.

The skills needed to adequately protect your wealth requires selecting the best people in their prospective fields. Just as you wouldn't allow a doctor to work on your car or a plumber to operate on your body, don't try to specialize in matters without having sufficient expertise. Instead, hire the best and let them help you with your goal. It cannot be overemphasis that the best will save you from avoidable errors, costly time and consequently wasted money. The intricacies of protecting your wealth and your to be wealth vary slightly from person to person depending on your goal.

To date, there are no infrastructures that endures the test of time, pressure and heat without a strong foundation. The same is true for wealth building. Failure to fully protect your assets is a grave mistake but building a legal wall around it is a mark of an intelligent person or institution. Like the skill of making money, protecting it also becomes second nature once the concept is properly understood. We already know that the educational system does not focus on the management of money nor the measures of protecting it. That type of tools are often shared among the top one percent of the world and all others have to essentially work for them. I, for one, am not okay with that arrangement. I will consider it a great progress if we can collectively elevate that number to sixty percent with each habitable continent having their fair share of ten. We can certainly achieve it through education.

You Must Learn

When one embarks on the initial journey of building wealth systems and becoming rich forever, the first and foremost agenda is to educate and orient oneself about the subject. Having a burning desire for wealth alone without immersing yourself in all its aspects is somewhat a gamble. Luck happens but it's very rare unless you do all you can to position yourself. How to position yourself is also illustrated in my eBook 5 Principles for Becoming Wealthy. It features The L. U. C. K. Y System and can be purchased on amazon but a free PDF version is available for all purchasers of this book. Simply visit DeviseWealth.com and download your copy.

Always try to look at things in various perspectives. For example, the nine-year-old boy Ghanaian that badly wanted to become an entrepreneur without any cash had to think outside the box. He quietly observed and realized that there is a bakery nearby that attracted long lines every morning. The remarkable thing was that although the demand was there, the people were often frustrated with the waiting and sometimes arguments ensued due to misunderstandings about one's position in the long line. Some people at the back of line often walked away without buying when they determine that the line is moving too slowly. Many have to go and catch transportation to work and they will be late if they spend too much time just to buy their daily bread.

He thought to himself, imagine how many more people opt out of coming to the bakery at all, due to these long lines condition. He had an aha moment so he decided to go throughout his neighborhood and conduct a simple research to see how many would like to buy bread in the morning if it was delivered to their doorstep. Although he knew that almost everyone enjoys eating bread with their tea, hot chocolate or porridge for breakfast, the result of the research was overwhelming. Realizing the opportunity and being a witness to this bakery's supply and demand problem, the boy talked to his mother about his intentions.

Later that afternoon during closing, this nine-year-old boy showed up at the bakery and greeted the owner. He introduces himself as Sister Julie's son and asked if he could talk to her about selling more bread every morning. The owner replied I have long lines here every day, haven't you seen? He told her that he had, and commented that he admires her because she has a great business. He asked if there were leftover bread at the end of the day. She replied yes, and said it was a result of not wanting to have shortages. She added, but then people sometimes leave without buying when the line is excessively long. Knowing that people preferred fresh bread and not leftovers from a previous day, the boy told her that he has a solution to reduce the number of leftovers without creating a shortage.

The young boy now has the owner's full attention. He explained that he would like to help by taking a tray of bread door to door and sell every morning before school. The lady demeanor gave the boy confidence that this is going to be a yes. Before she could say a word, the boy showed her a two page paper of consensus, full of names and preferred type of bread that the people would buy. She asked, did you go to all these people houses? The boy replied, yes ma'am. He added, my mother does not have any money to buy the bread in bulk so he would like to sell it for tips if he does a good job. Without even discussing any commission rate of pay or anything, she asked the boy to begin the next morning. A big smile engulfed all of the young boy's face.

He would have to be there by 5:30 am to pull this off and still make it to school by 8:00 am. Needless to say, the boy was punctual the very next day and his journey began as a problem solver and an entrepreneur. Since then he's gone on and solved many other problems. I'm proud to say that I knew this young nine-year-old boy very well because he is I. What started as a tip for selling bread became ten percent and I remember vividly when the owner explained to me what ten percent was. She simply said you will get the price of 1 bread for every 10 bread you sell. With that, I knew without a doubt how to calculate my daily earnings.

You see, I learned by observing, researching and thinking outside the box as a young boy. In essence, I had negotiated to sell on consignment and commission without knowing the terms or what they meant. I then planned a simple yet effective system and process that ended up making me money over and over again. At the core, I built an asset in the form of a business. I had my friends do the same thing the following year in different neighborhoods in exchange for a small commission from the bakery owner. The system worked for other ventures as I even took it a step further and began selling kerosene in the evening since most people at the time used kerosene lamps. Before long, I gave opportunities to my friends once again by having them sell kerosene for me but this time I gave the commission. I even continued to collect commissions from my friend's effort several weeks without working. It was during a period when I was assembling my neighborhood little league soccer team. I was thirteen.

Although I left the country when I was only 15, I made significant impact and contribution to my community by providing 2 highly demanded products and building a small business around it. I had every intention of one day buying my own bakery because I saw an endless demand for bread. The question of selling kerosene would have ended at some point as more and more people begun to get access to electricity. Anyway, I managed to seek understanding of a common problem and created a solution and that is the very essence of a business.

The systems and processes that were used then are still relevant today. Learn all you can about whatever business or investment endeavor that you wish to undertake. This will give you a clear sense of direction and comfortability as you pursue your goals of asset acquisition. When you learn, you are also more susceptible to asking the important questions. Mistakes are avoided or kept to a minimum. Recruitment of the very best people for formulating your team becomes second nature. Your level of competence will show as you deal with experienced people within your team and in the industry as a whole. Finally, you'll be respected as an authority in your field by your staff, customers, business partners, and your community. You simply have to learn before you earn so in the event all is lost, you can start all over again without hesitation.

Why Many People are not Rich

If you're not able to effectively manage your resources for building wealth, you simply need a mindset shift and seek more financial education. There's absolutely nothing wrong with not knowing as long as you know that you don't know. When one is aware, that person can begin to take steps to change their circumstances. You have to believe because not believing that you can be rich is an enemy within. Every nonbeliever has their own unique reason but I can assure you that absolutely anyone can be rich.

It starts with believing. Believe it in your core, your soul, and with all your heart. Not believing get you nowhere, however, there's a level of commitment that transcends into actions when one accepts or feels sure about something. The feeling that you can be rich is one that only you can invite. Be realistic and conduct some soul searching and if you conclude that you just don't have what it takes, ask yourself why. Challenging yourself will sometimes unmask the truth which can enable you to make whatever adjustments that are needed. Re-examine again after some time to see if you now believe. Often after this exercise, there's a change of heart.

The second reason is not learning how to be rich. You've never been rich before so you must learn. Before a child could walk and talk, that child had to learn. Granted, the child may have fallen a few times but that did not deter the child from trying. They learned and now getting around is a breeze. Learn how to become rich and becoming rich will be as easy as walking. Study someone that is rich by following their work and reaching out to them for mentorship when feasible. Feel free to get all the free publications and if it's truly helping you, do not hesitate to purchase their products for sale. It's a win-win because you get the insight needed and support your mentor at the same time. For instance, when you have seriously applied the systems I'm teaching here and need additional assistance, feel free to reach out to me. I have other products and services that will take you by the hand and show a more intimate step by step process.

Not taking steps towards becoming rich is the third reason. One of the most natural thing a person can do is apply the lessons they've learned, so it's therefore unusual not to do so. Begin your quest for building wealth. Start small and set goals to grow at various milestones. Continue to increase your efforts and watch your wealth expand like a balloon. I assure you, it's a beautiful thing but you've got to start the process. When you compare the daunting task of going to work for someone for 40 years versus having your own system of wealth building that will free you from any employer, the decision should be quite easy.

The fourth reason is failure to protect your assets. No one stands tall all by themselves. Reach out for assistance when you need it. Don't follow anyone unless they themselves have the proper protective mechanisms in place. In other words, get advice from only competent people. A rule of thumb is to protect everything that is of significant value to you.

Not repeating the process is the final reason why people are not rich. It takes duplicating your wealth systems as often as possible to become rich. After you have believed, learned, taken steps, got yourself a mentor, and are starting to see growth in your wealth, you must repeat or expand the process. Make it bigger, higher, better, faster and smarter. You've accomplished something great so why stop there. Whatever the challenges may be, you can install systems to simplify, automate, cut cost and make things smoother the next time around. As long as you have realized a sizable gain, you should expand it. Conquer these 5 reasons why people are not rich and you'll become rich. Yes, you can, after all, you are an asset.

The Purpose of an Asset

First of all, let's not make any mistake about it, you are an asset. Your very existence and whatever physical, mental, spiritual capabilities you possess are all tools that can be utilized to acquire more assets. To properly use the tools that you already possess, one must have a clear understanding of who they are, what they seek to achieve and how to bring it to fruition. When these factors are properly defined, one would have already begun on the journey of financial education. The key is to realize that you are an asset and you must make a decision to acquire more assets. Even the person that has no money, no job, and no savings are just as much of an asset as the person that has much more.

What is the definition of an asset, one may ask? An asset is anyone or anything of value. Ethically, anyone can be hired, contracted or utilized to help create more value but for the anything part, it can and should be acquired solely to create more value. At an absolute minimum, an asset is a person or thing that has the potential of generating value that can be converted into money or cash flow as I use the terms interchangeably. Therefore no matter what your circumstances may be, your trajectory is already destined to make money and that is the purpose of an asset. If you're not satisfied with how much money you make, then you will have to tap into the other assets mentioned above. The concept of getting more assets is simple but it must truly resonate with you before proceeding. Measures to protect your assets before you get it and beyond will be explained in the coming chapters.

An asset in its simplest form consists of two factors. These two factors when properly understood will make a big difference going forward. I will explain. In the paragraph above, I mentioned that asset makes you money. What if your first asset does not make sufficient money to meet your goal? Well, you will have to buy more assets. The more assets you utilize or acquire, the more money you generate. If becoming rich is your desire, it makes no sense to take on liabilities. Exhaust every option possible to use debt in all your asset acquisition with the exception of a down payment or administration cost.

Look at it this way, an asset is the total of liability plus equity. Liability is what you owe, a negative number, and equity is what you own, a positive number. In fact, beside shelter, food, clothing, transportation, utilities and a few other essential things for your family, which are all liabilities, everything else that you buy should be an asset if you intend on becoming and staying rich. Equity is nice but always acquire assets that produce cash flow. That said, if you have an asset that does not lead to more cash flow, it's time to make a change.

More often than not, those that say all their bills are necessities and therefore have no allowance to buy assets may have a change of heart after careful examination of their lifestyle. Even those that maintain that money wasted is insignificant, after having exposure of what it could have become, may also rethink their position. The fact remains that money spent on liabilities die an immediate death and never grows. Money invested is assets, however, have a great probability to grow, sometimes exponentially if done intelligently.

You can enjoy yourself and splurge a little when you reach a certain status of wealth. Reaching this level is not luck by any stretch of imagination. There are proven mindset, methods, and strategies that must be employed. Conditioning yourself to clearly distinguish the difference between what makes and cost you money is mandatory. Positioning yourself to invest in what makes you money is necessary.

The minute your earnings begin to increase, you must protect it. Protecting your asset begins with correctly structuring it. You, as an asset, must incorporate a business in order to take advantage of the multitude of protections currently available. More on protecting your asset will be covered in chapter 3. Capital or initial funding is needed to start any business. The amount required is directly related to the type of business one wishes to establish. While some may entail just a few hundred dollars to get started, others will necessitate having a few thousand, tens of thousands or even hundreds of thousands. The idea is to use little money to get big credit for any business venture or acquisition. A leverage mindset is what is needed to facilitate the money and credit ratio to pull this off.

Money and the utilization of it, date back to several thousand years before the Common Era (BCE). Ancient civilized people of which is now Ethiopia, Sudan, and Egypt used things of perceived value through a barter system to trade with others in the region and along the Nile River. It is important to point out that some places used the weight of grain to justify precious metal such as gold. The takeaway is that money is whatever value the people collectively accept. Anyway, later came the emergence of a stamped unit in the form of metals, then paper to lighten the load. Stamped money in the form of metal was used as early as 700 BC.

Today, the dollar is the official monetary unit of many countries like the United States of America, Canada, Australia, Hong Kong, New Zealand and others. Its origin dates back to the year 1520 when silver was minted in the Czech Republic and later lent its name to other similar coins. The American dollar is one of the most recognized bill of treasure in the world. Unit of weighted gold that was once used to back paper money was officially removed by the United States in 1973. Credit is now the king.

When you have money, you are able to afford things that otherwise you would do without. All good deeds in our society can be multiplied when you have lots of money. Almost everything we do here on earth requires money, so it is imperative that we understand how to grow it. Acquire assets to grow your money then use it to get more assets and as the cycle continues you become richer for it.

Becoming Wealthy from the Bottom-up

Let's define the bottom in terms of finances for the purpose of the subject, shall we? My functional adult brothers and sisters in the human family who do not own a house and or have an income source. One with no credit or bad credit and currently in debt from student loans, medical bills, credit cards or other forms of liabilities. My beloved young folks that may have opted out of continuing higher education, current college students, or recent graduates that have not planned out their financial future. You are all my people and I'll do my best to help you.

The primary thing that has to be done is conditioning yourself for the wealth. Although it may sound far-fetched, it is not. In fact, simply replacing self-doubt with belief and confidence is the first step. Not knowing that you can do it should be replaced with a mindset of how can I do it. Take an inventory of five people you know that are doing better than you financially, five you've seen, anywhere that appears to have their financial affairs in order, and five you've heard of but have not seen, that are wealthy. Ask yourself if any of them are more worthy than you. I'll answer that for you, no. With determination, you too can create wealth for yourself and your family.

When you believe you can achieve wealth, you have to seek how. Educating yourself is extremely important as you cannot have any level of continued success without a proven system. Experienced people and institutions have been there, and done that. Many challenges have already be crossed and conquered. The outcome is the formulation of systems that help avoid pitfalls and minimize the learning curve. These systems often include best practices and the fastest way to reach our dreams. Attach yourself to such people or institution and absorb all you can. In most cases, educators such as myself spray knowledge in forms of E-books, books, blogs, videos, webinars, membership sites, seminars, training courses, live coaching, newsletters and other publications. The good news is that most of the value offered are all free. When you get great value from the free material and need more, it is then okay to invest in yourself by seeking paid products and services. There's nothing better than knowing the value of something before you get it.

Believing and learning means absolutely nothing without application in the area of wealth creation. This is a subject that involves action. Taking calculated steps towards building your own wealth is vital and creates a momentum that once started becomes semi-automatic. Your efforts begin to materialize and you begin to get richer than you were previously. The system of principles that guides wealth building makes it easier to elevate and duplicate at exponential levels and within 5 to 10 years' time, you can have a substantial amount of money from assets that require very little attention from you personally. Much more money than the average household income in the United States.

Beware, the minute you begin to get rich comes people that want to take it from you. Consequently, you have to be smart and install defense mechanisms to protect yourself and your assets. Do not forsake this important action as it can bite you pretty hard and set you back unnecessarily. Avoid this mistake so you save yourself time and money. It is not difficult to protect yourself but people often forget it and only realize after falling victim to these takers. They come in all shapes and sizes and do not fit into any one character but are deterred when they see that their attempts will be useless.

As I mentioned previously, you must repeat the process that produces gains. This is equally as important. Now that you've conquered the belief system, excelled in the learning department, capitalized on the wealth building at some level, and have asset protection in place, it is now time to do it again on a larger scale. Continue to repeat the process and enjoy it thoroughly on your way up to where the wealthy resides.

Money Mindset for Success

Although we all use money, we sometimes don't fully understand it. It is often not what people think it is. Money is only valuable because we say it is. We are confident when the economy is good. This is one of the reasons why currencies from countries with a thriving economy are valued higher than those without and vice versa. If any economy dives into a depression for an extended period of time, their currency will likely weaken. If any attempts to remedy it involves printing too much money by the federal reserves, it will lead to inflation which later leads to the devaluation of that currency.

The take away is that money can come and go so your wealth should not be defined by how much money you have. A million dollars today could be worth five hundred thousand in a very short period of time with severe inflation. Knowing this, it is important that you understand how to maintain and exercise the proper money mindset for success. Below are just a few money mindsets that when adopted will create an increase in your quest to create or build wealth.

1. Money is a subject that has to be understood and mastered

2. Money must be transformed into an income producing asset

3. Money is most efficient when it moves around

4. Money should be used as leverage

5. Money should be used as arbitrage

6. Money is not the root of evil

7. Money should work for you, not you for money

I am a big proponent of correct, relevant and useful education. Life is much easier that way and in matters of finances, that sentiment certainly applies. Learn all you can about money. What it is and how to grow it. The most effective way to use it should also be of interest to you. As a matter of fact, studying what wealthy people do with their money will serve as an additional clue. Examine the clues and see how they apply to you.

Attitude towards money often changes when one begins to learn and understand that it is just a medium of exchange. The exchange itself is what is important. That is why money must be transformed into a thing of value such as profitable businesses, passive income real estates, dividend producing investments and ventures with great ROI. (Return on investment) As low as the banks pay on interest from savings, no one would be happy if they suddenly stopped paying it. In the same sense, people should not be happy if their money yields zero return no matter where it is stored. What I mean to convey to you is that you should actively look for ways to make your money grow. Some of the best ways to increase your funds are to acquire real estate, a business, or an investment. That is how to transform your money into income-producing assets.

Even if you have a job, it would be wise if you take a portion of your income and move it into an asset. There are so many reasons not to rely on a job but I'll save that for another day. Buying the right asset means cash flow for a very long time. The movement of money into asset will produce money for you to spend in the first place. It is a continuous cycle that when grown and nurtured properly will make you very rich. It does not make sense to have money idle anywhere in the long term so the equity in your home is of no use to you. With financial education, things will become clear and you'll take it out and put it to work for your benefit.

One of the reasons why I decided to become an educator and share my financial knowledge is because a lot of my family members and friends had no idea that they had money sitting idle and worse what they could do about it. It saddened me every time but gave me joy when they understood what they could do after I explained it to them. The biggest area of confusion is the equity in their homes. Yes, you want to pay off your mortgage but have that equity worked for you. Even in the process of paying off your home, the equity there can actually be used to produce more income, which can be used to accelerate your payoff if you so desired. Wherever your money lives, make it active by acquiring an asset and you will see an increase.

In the last decade or so I have had the opportunity of educating people financially and I have found that many just don't use leverage. Some as a result of not knowing how while others never thought of it. You can't build wealth on any noticeable measure without the use of leverage. Every quest to create wealth should include leveraging your money for more money. Whether you need to start a business, buy into Real Estate or make other forms of investment, use leverage by borrowing the majority of your money from a lender.

Of course, there are requirements that must be met such as good credit, collateral, income etc., however, that is nothing compared to what you stand to lose if you use your own money entirely. One example I gave earlier was using one hundred thousand dollars to buy five rental houses by leveraging your money as opposed to maybe buying just one. Maximize your capacity for earning by ways of leverage.

Another mistake I see a lot of new investors make is not using arbitrage. You must constantly look at the opportunity cost of investing in one thing as opposed to the other. When you see an imbalance, go for the one that yields a higher return assuming they have the same amount of risk. For instance, buying 20 rental houses rather than buying a 20 unit apartment complex is lack of using arbitrage. If you accumulated the 20 units over time then it's okay however eventually selling them all to acquire the 20 unit complex is a better use of arbitrage if all the factors are the same or similar. For sure, the benefits of operating and maintaining your property in one place are innumerable.

Money is not the root of all evil. Erase that nonsense from your mind if you think that way. Money makes it possible to enjoy life at a greater level and help people beyond your imagination. It can create enormous wealth if utilized correctly and solves lots of life problems. It gives you comfort, security, and peace of mind when you transform it into income-producing assets. It's actually the opposite of evil as it can help you fight evil should the need arise. If it were the root of all evil, you wouldn't need it just to survive in today's world.

We have all done this at one point or another but hopefully, after reading, viewing and practicing the lesson here, you'll see all the benefits of having money work for you and proceed to treat it accordingly. When you make the mistake of working for money, it could become a lifetime sentence but you can emancipate yourself and make money work for you instead. Money can be more efficient as it doesn't need any rest or break. You don't have to pay it and it's not unethical to work it twenty-four hours a day. No matter what your circumstance may be, with a little shift in money mindset and some financial education, you'll see the need to reverse your relationship with money. You'll make money work for you unapologetically.

Credit Mindset for Success

You might have heard stories of people around you taking on moderate to major ventures with no real personal capital. You might have wondered how they did it. It was credit. Success in wealth creation is much easier when you have access to credit. When this factor is properly understood, it becomes a mindset that causes one to act in accordance with utilizing credit every chance they get. It's OPM (other people's money) and you can borrow more of it than you have at your disposal. This is because the lender looks at your net worth and your cash at hand in the financial statement and will lend you significantly more than you have in cash. It makes absolutely no sense to use your own money to undertake a venture.

Credit is now more important than ever, especially now that money itself is no longer backed by precious metals in arguably the strongest nation in the world. We as a society have been catapulted into consuming at a higher rate, but the sad thing is that those that aren't financially literate, consume to make others rich. When people suddenly begin to see the full picture, they will most likely make changes to the way they spend especially when using credit. Let me list a few credit mindset for success that accelerates the wealth creation process.

1. Credit is a subject that has to be understood and mastered

2. Credit is a privilege

3. Credit should be embraced, not feared

4. Credit is easy to build with discipline

5. Credit grows when you strategize properly

6. Credit is more powerful than money

7. Credit should be used to acquire assets, not liabilities

If you do not have great credit, there are measures you can take to reverse your situation as I will provide many processes of accomplishing that in the next chapter. Just like money, credit is also a subject that has to be studied and mastered. Any real ambition of wealth without credit is not optimized, but the marriage of money and credit makes the impossible possible in terms of reach. One who learns what credit represents and how to best use it to enrich themselves has an advantage over those that simply use it for funding useless things.

I can assure you that If you are nineteen years or older and do not have a FICO credit score of at least 785, you do not understand credit. Getting great credit is not difficult, it requires discipline, free of impulse buying and paying your bills on time. In fact, a golden nugget rule is to have money but use credit to pay instead. Once that transaction takes place, you have thirty days to pay it in full. This exercise alone will do wonders for your credit health and set you above seventy-five percent of the population.

The misconception is that because people are bombarded with credit card offers through mails and in the departmental stores etc., they often feel as if credit is their right. That is far from the truth. Credit is a privilege and it can be taken from you and set you back tremendously if not cared for as such. In that case, not having credit at all is better and easier to build than having horrible credit through negligence. That said, however, all hope is not lost as there are many remedies that can be utilized towards an expedient path of bad credit correction. It will not be as effective without the correct mindset, therefore, first thing has to be first when your circumstances have submerged you under water.

Other than irresponsible use, the credit card should definitely be embraced, not feared. We all know the power of earth, wind, and fire, not the musical group but the actual. These things can all kill you instantly but can also be used to preserve life. To a lesser degree, a man-made tool such as a knife and a gun can also be used to take a life or protect a life. The difference lies between who has it and what their intentions are for it. The utilization determines if it is safe or unsafe in an individual's possession. With a deep understanding of what it can do for you and to you, the respect will be there and you'll likely embrace it rather than fear it.

It is so easy to build credit following the proper steps, any eighteen years old man or woman can do it. I just don't agree with the school's systems not teaching this very crucial part of life skills. This should definitely be in the curriculum of all schools right alongside money. Parents have to do their part as well and pave the way so that they can teach and exercise building credit with their 18-year-olds. Just a simple add-on to one credit card of a financially responsible adult will start the education and building process for these teenagers. Those that lack that option can do it on their own, with a secured credit card after learning about credit, and feeling as if they are matured enough to handle the responsibility.

Again don't get enticed by the notion of free money and get yourself all confused. Your approach should be, to reach a near perfect credit. Upon completion of basic credit education, you can use credit along with some savings to acquire your first cash-producing asset. If I can get the twenty-five percent of the eighteen-year-old to think with this type of mindset, the goal of expanding the wealthy one percent to sixty percent fairly worldwide across all the 6 useful continents would be inevitable. Having the correct mindset means they will teach their children as well.

Develop strategies for growing your credit. It will afford you larger undertakings of assets which of course means more wealth. Assets appreciate in value over time and it is great, however, the right ones produce cash flow automatically and can render you true financial freedom. I'm talking about freedom from having to be an employee, freedom from time constraints, freedom from being stuck in one place and freedom from bad health and cheap lifestyle among many others. The minute you figure out that your actions as a result of learning that credit is profitable, you'll actively seek to expand it by maximizing your unique strategies.

Many think that money is more powerful than credit. On the contrary, credit is the one with an edge. The impression that money is more powerful may be a result of people being able to physically touch it, while credit is more subtle. They view cash as tangible but fail to see credit in the same light. The truth is credit is much more powerful and can do much more than its partner, cash. I still maintain that they are paired, in the quest for becoming rich.

For the life of me, I do not understand why people use credit to buy bad debt and struggle to keep up when the other option is much more viable and makes you rich. Stop buying liabilities with credit. Start buying assets with credit and before long, you'll be financially independent of anything and anyone. That to me is total freedom. It is not complicated but it does require learning and application.

Leverage Mindset for Success

Imagine a co-worker with the same income and economic opportunities as you. After taking a closer look at their financial statement, you found that they own a business or a rental real estate and generating a sizable additional income as a result. More than likely, this person is using leverage and you can do the same thing. Whenever something is used to maximize advantages, it is referred to as leverage. You can find leverage all around you and maybe even uses it without thinking about it. The focus of this section, however, is the leverage of becoming wealthy. It entails using resources at your disposal to advance your agenda of building wealth. It could be a partnership venture, debt, and systems of instruments, expertise, or other human resources. If it can help you attain your goal of becoming rich, it is leverage. Reading this book and applying the systems outlined here is a form of leverage. It simply cuts time, money, effort, and learning curve in financial matters.

Everyone uses it but not many know the proper application and ramification of leverage. If you take one hundred percent of your own money to purchase or finance a business, you have failed to use leverage. Likewise doing extended but less significant task in your basket of tasks is not leverage. Manually doing something that can be done with a tool at a much higher efficiency is the absence of leverage. Trying to do your own business taxes or draw your own legal documents when a competent professional can do it properly and save you time and money, in the long run, is negligence of leverage.

Trying to create wealth without knowing how when there are wealthy people to model, financial educators to follow, and publications to absorb is leverage abandonment. The numerical leverage mindset below, if adopted will propel you to the next level in terms of building wealth.

1. Leverage is a subject that has to be understood and mastered

2. Leverage is using more of other people resources (OPR)

3. Leverage should be utilized for wealth at all cost

4. Leverage is more powerful than your money alone

5. Leverage is more powerful than your credit alone

6. Leverage should be used to acquire assets not liabilities

7. Leverage is a team sport

Financial education once again is knocking at your door. Do not ignore it as it will give you an unfair advantage over those that remain isolated from the knowledge. Face it head on and learn the appropriate uses of leverage. As you continue to learn, you'll become more and more comfortable and when you begin to apply the lessons, you'll gain more insight and begin to accumulate experience. I would start small and do larger undertakings as time progress.

If you have a house with equity and have not used it to enrich yourself by pulling it to buy assets that produce cash flow, you have not learned nor mastered leverage. Money should never be given any rest. It does not sleep and leaving it idle is the absent of leverage because you are letting money sleep when it does not need it. As you can see, learning and mastering all things leverage in matters of wealth creation should be a prime focus.

We live in a connected world and no one could survive happily for an extended period of time without human connection, bond, and association. We lean on our folk for conversation, socialization, and even at times validation. Occasionally when faced with complex challenges, we seek advice from members in our closest circle. We partner with other adult of our taste and compatibility to start a family. Those are all a form of leverage because it makes life better for us.

Using more of other people resources in whatever capacity needed for mutual benefit is leverage at its finest. If you've followed my work, you would know that I applied leverage at a tender age of nine years without even knowing the word or its definition. Not having any money, I negotiated with a nearby bakery to allow me to sell bread throughout my neighborhood for a tip. The tip later turned into a ten percent commission. This small initiative of leverage gave me an opportunity to earn money and later became one of the building blocks of my financial acumen.

You are reading this book because you are interested in building wealth. If you're like me, you'll likely read it twice to fully grasp the essence of the systems I'm teaching. Then again some are able to grasp the concept right away and run with it. Knowing that I have a diverse group of audience, I try to write in a simple yet engaging style while releasing key points such as mindsets, principles, benefits and how to, all encapsulated into proven systems of wealth. In a way, I'm using leverage to teach what many go to college for four years and never get. Using leverage for wealth at all cost is not a subject thought in schools. The reason is simple, our educational institution has their own agenda and it is to produce workers, not wealthy people.

Money and credit alone pales in comparison to the power of leverage. Through leverage, however, you can use the combination to reach greater heights in terms of borrowing power. A sound business person or entity with a lot of access to lending by way of leverage will produce magnificent returns. So money is good and credit is even better but leverage is the icing on the cake. Leverage is seeking and recognizing opportunities wherever they exist and using it to further your gain.

Identifying leverage in its various form is not that difficult and sometimes causes people to misuse it. Only use leverage to acquire assets. Never use it for liabilities. When you have accumulated enough assets to a good level and it begins to bear fruits, you are then free to indulge since the wealth system is already in place. Business offline and/or online, real estate, and investments are all playground for tremendous success in becoming wealthy using leverage.

Finally, leverage is a team sport and should be treated as such. For instance, when you set out to start an offline business, you'll need to conduct product, customer, location, staffing and operational research among others. Without a team, this tasks may seem daunting and overwhelm you before the establishment is completed. Due to the leverage of a team, however, responsibilities are shared in an organized fashion that the process forms smoothly without any major setback or oversight. Use a team of competent professionals as leverage each time you embark on any wealth building journey.

Asset Protection Mindset for Success

What if your personal and business assets can be safeguarded so the probability of losing any accumulated wealth, at any point, to any circumstances in your life is slim to none, would you not want to know how? I'm sure you would and the answer is embedded in the fact that all things of value must be protected. Athletes protect themselves in the event of an injury. Singers take protective measures for their voices should something happen to their vocal cords. Dancers protect their legs knowing they cannot dance without them. Many of us are mandated to protect our homes, cars, and health with insurances. When you are in possession of something valuable such as your life and other assets, the sentiment of protection should remain high on your radar. To put it another way, if you cannot afford to lose it, protect it.

The question of asset protection is extremely important for those that aspire to build wealth and those that are already in progress. The process of wealth creation takes strategic thinking and partners as well as a variety of resources. Any neglect of a crucial step can slow or reverse the process. As you know, there's the learning factor and the application but a third and most often forgotten is asset protection. Although many know they should, a vast majority do it inadequately while a small group fails to take any measures at all. It is a tragedy for anyone to work hard and build a valuable entity only to lose it to theft, lawsuit, loss and so forth.

From the very beginning of your journey, there must be a clear and solid roadmap. This document should define what you want to accomplish and how to do so. It must state a starting point with milestones along the way. Built-in protection should be activated when necessary as the plan proceeds. Some have to be present from day one while others can be added as time goes on. Your goal in the first place is to become wealthy so take actions to ensure it remains that way. Below, you'll discover some very important asset protection mindset for success:

1. Asset protection is a subject that has to be understood and mastered

2. Asset protection should be used to guard your tangible and intangible assets

3. Asset protection is separating yourself from your wealth by incorporating

4. Asset protection means having adequate insurances

5. Asset protection is compartmentalizing but staying in control

6. Asset protection should include a lawyer, CPA, insurance agent, and security company

7. Asset protection must be reviewed yearly for any oversight

There you have it. This compressed list of mindset in regards to asset protection should pertain to everyone and organizations that aspire for profit. The absence of these important mechanisms could very well put any business under. Let's say for an example a young entrepreneur named John owns a small coffee shop and a house. The house has some equity and homeowners insurance. Meanwhile, the business is a DBA (doing business as) and also lack general liability insurance. One day a customer accidentally spilled hot coffee on his lap and suffered a burn. He sues John and the case is awaiting litigation. What do you think will happen in this case? Many attorneys will take the case on contingency fees, meaning they'll only get paid if their client wins. These attorneys can operate this way because they evaluate cases to see if there are assets without protection they can go after. Consequently, if

John loses the case, he will likely get a charging order against him that can wipe him out of a business and equity in his home.

How sad would that be when John could have taken just two more step and spend six to nine hundred dollars to legally separate his personal assets from his business plus added general liability insurance. Had that occurred, the judgment would have only reached the limits of the GL insurance. John would still have a business and equity in his home. This unfortunate scenario is just a case of low hanging fruit. John could have taken asset protection to another level by taking equity out of his home every few years. That money could have made profit from assets under a properly structured entity.

As you can see, the need for a sound mindset in asset protection is very important when you have things of value. Simple precaution and a little investment for safeguarding your assets will save you an unnecessary loss in the litigious society of today. If you take extreme care in protecting your assets, it would actually serve as a deterrent and lawyers will refuse to take the case on contingency fees. The would-be plaintiff, most likely wouldn't want to pay lawyer fees upfront, so they'll be more likely open to remedies other than a lawsuit.

Tax Savings Mindset for Success

When a large portion of your hard earned money is taxed and you discover that others legally pay the least minimum to nothing at all, you should want to know why. Because taxes are taken before you are paid as employees, many just don't feel the loss. Thirty percent or more gone and it is done so tactfully that people don't care to see if there's something that can be done to remedy it. Then you become privy to information that suggest that tax code, in general, is written to allow tax breaks for people that provide jobs, housing, food, and energy. The breaks and deductions are so enormous that a company could end up paying absolutely nothing once they've taken advantage of all the tax savings allowed by law.

Every effort should be made to unmask the tax code. Becoming a beneficiary of such savings cannot be far from anyone agenda especially if wealth is your primary focus. It does not mean that you have to thoroughly understand it after reading. Many just don't have the background required to gain full comprehension, however, your tax accountant should. A collaboration between your CPA and your business attorney will result in a tax savings strategy designed for your unique undertaking. There is no need to try and figure it out on your own and take chances that may result in a penalty. Using your team's extensive knowledge and focusing on other things is a solid advice when wealth creation is your goal. The following are 7 tax savings mindset for success.

1. Tax savings is a subject that has to be understood and mastered

2. Tax savings should not be strategized without a CPA and corporate attorney

3. Tax savings is most beneficial to passive income business owners

4. Tax savings is least beneficial to people whose only income is ordinary

5. Tax savings requires organization and proper documentation

6. Tax savings benefit businesses that use contractors instead of employees

7. Tax savings is beneficial when business and personal finances are separate

Listen casually to your friends about life and personal matters but when it comes to the subject of tax savings, it is better to get information from your certified public accountant and corporate lawyer. These two professionals possess expert knowledge and experience, therefore, they can formulate optimal strategy collectively for your agenda. You can learn quite a bit by reading the tax code for yourself, however, mastering it will begin to take root as you collaborate with your tax team.

Your corporate attorney and CPA are going to apply the tax code strategically as it pertains to the business that you undertake. A real estate venture for example will include tax deductions such as depreciation, interest on loans, other business expenses and a plan for tax deferment in case of a sale through what is known as a 1031 exchange. Remember that depreciation is spread over a course of twenty-seven years. All repairs up to two thousand five hundred dollars in cost are deductible expense. Not knowing this could mean leaving lots of money on the table.

A person with a business venture however will take other tax deductions such as health premiums and care. This person can take tax deduction for things such as parties, gifts, vacation, clothes, tuition, car and even pay up to five thousand five hundred dollars each for their children under eighteen years as employees.

The icing on the cake is that the kids pay no taxes on these earnings either. The compensation can be for any duties that they perform within the business, and proper documentation is the key. There are many more and it would be a shame to miss them as a result of failure to consult with your tax team.

Passive income earners will benefit more than ordinary income earners. Aside from all the tax savings mentioned above, there are others such as fifty-five cents a mile allowance allowed for travel as long as its business related. Keeping a log is a sure way to stay organized and avoid confusion. None of the tax savings mentioned above is possible for anyone who is just an employee. That person's ordinary income is taxed the highest with no room for relief.

So the take away is that ordinary income earners are the most taxed people. They don't have any employees, no business, no real estate, no investments, and therefore not a viable candidate for any tax breaks. If you fall into this category and you own a home and have children, you can at least have those two deductions but it pales in comparison with that of the passive and portfolio income earners.

If you have a business that can operate with independent contractors as opposed to employees, it is smart to do it that way. It simplifies the process and saves a lot of money in the long run. For instance, a business will just issue an IRS form1099 to everyone paid and that's the end of its responsibility. On the other hand, having employees means payroll deductions. You also have to match each employee's social security and Medicare deductions, plus withholding federal and in some cases state taxes. All of these funds have to be sent in for taxes along with the proper filling documents. Contractor or not, tax savings is most beneficial to passive income business owners.

Build Wealth Forever in Just 5 Years

You have officially been lied to if you were told that taking thirty years to pay off your mortgage is the best way to go. It is indeed one way but not the best in any stretch of imagination. If you find yourself in that type of rat race, there's still hope of building wealth. You can adopt a strategy of using the equity in the home to acquire more assets for profit. You'll then repeat the process whenever possible and wealth will begin to accumulate but at a slow pace. It is good but there are better options.

Pay off your house in 5 years and you now have the entire equity of your home to use as a means of wealth creation. Simultaneously, your credit will also increase astronomically so that at the end of the payoff, you are placed in the finest position of attaining the best loan for your wealth creation. Apply leverage to this large equity and credit that you now possess, and lenders will literally throw money at you. You are in a position to negotiate terms and interest of the loan. Only a few segments of the population has this type of option. Building wealth forever in just five years is very possible so long as you know how. It requires knowledge, discipline, and coaching.

Without knowledge of wealth systems, the probability of pulling it off is slim. This task requires learning about money, credit, leverage, asset protection, and repeating the process but at a higher level each time. A team has to be installed that includes a mentor that is already wealthy or has started building wealth. Occasional one on one interactions would be necessary to assess milestones and make adjustments. Other team members will include a corporate attorney, an accountant, a real estate agent and a loan officer.

A level of discipline and accountability would be vital as well. A person who wishes to build wealth in 5 years has to stay focus and keep their eyes on the prize. Habits such as impulse buying, unnecessary liabilities and lack of control have to be suppressed. There will be plenty of time later to consume and indulge but during the wealth creation process, strict routines and actions have to be followed.

Each phase of the process should be co-monitored by an experienced mentor or coach. The purpose is to ensure smoothness and also catch any oversight that might occur. The coach will be the one to ask the hard questions, give critique and provide guidance throughout as you pass through the milestones of the wealth process. Coaching is supplemental and should not be substituted with the actual training required to build real wealth.

The process of building wealth in 5 years begins on day one of your mortgage payment. This strategy has built-in capital, great credit, leverage potential, arbitrage, asset protection as well as real estate, investment and business ventures. The accelerated nature of this plan enables quick equity growth which in turn is leverage for a business loan by the second year. A portion of the profits earned from a carefully vetted business will then be re-invested in other ventures including real estate, paper assets, and other businesses. Of course, arbitrage will be utilized when selecting which venture to undertake next.

In five years' time, the home is fully paid off and the equity from both the business, the primary home as well as the rental home and other investment can all be leveraged in acquiring a larger venture. It can be a commercial rental real estate such as an apartment complex that is fully occupied and producing a great NOI (net operating income) or another profitable business. It can also be both depending on the net worth and other indicators the financial statement.

When executed correctly, you would potentially have at least 2 single family homes, a duplex, triplex or fourplex if you're able to get it. You will also have a profitable business or two under your management and/or a commercial real estate building. All of these assets will produce cash and the cycle continues. No one will complain at this point if you now enjoy some of the proceeds as you've assembled a machine that will continue to generate profits indefinitely.

Multiple Streams of Income

The primary objective of creating wealth is to acquire abundance of cash flow. As part of the overall system of generating wealth, multiple streams of income should be at the forefront. A set up that allows various built-in paths to earning income, re-enforces the structure and hence more cash flow. Not having it is basically putting all your eggs in one basket. It is not wise as there's no absolute certainty. We take calculated risk based on education and understanding of the product or service as well as the historical performances and trends. Other indicators include evaluation, quality, demand, due diligence, vision, and an experienced competent team to execute. Yet with all these aggregations of data, unforeseen elements could slow the progress of the wealth building process.

Having multiple streams of income establishes a comfort zone that enables branching into other ventures. It safeguards against industry fluctuations and works as a hedge when a downturn occurs in certain areas. At the same time, it increases net worth and opens doors into bigger ventures and acquisitions. The groundwork takes time and precision but if done correctly, there are many benefits to enjoy.

Other areas include on and offline businesses, real estate, and paper asset investments. There are so many profitable opportunities in these areas for those that have the knowledge, experience and the team. More often than not, these areas can be artificially inter-connected depending on the specific product or service. Build your business with the type of thinking that everything must be installed on the surface of real estate. The case for real estate itself and offline business is certainly plain to see but the same holds true for online businesses. It is a virtual real estate with billions of potential customers. The cost to have a piece of it can be zero or at your own set price. You read it right. There are many opportunities for making consistent money online without a website, a software, ads, or any other tool that otherwise would cost money. A serious business person, however, would quickly graduate into a structure with systems of wealth that requires some capital investment.

Like online, there are no shortages of profitable options for offline businesses. It takes more capital in most cases to construct. The mentality is not how much it takes necessarily but the earning potential. Getting the resources needed would not be difficult if the business plan is comprehensive and demonstrate profitability. With money, credit, and leverage, the business is likely to get funded. For these reasons, asking how much can be made is a better question, as opposed to how much does it cost.

Whenever possible, offline businesses should include real estate. Try to avoid leasing a space to operate. Paying someone else mortgage while they enjoy all the tax benefits, appreciation, and cash flow is not something to take great pleasure in. Constructing or buying your own building increases your net worth and affords you all the benefits mentioned above in addition to your business itself. It's the best way to approach an offline business. Real estate simply adds many other benefits and value to businesses like no other.

Your streams of income are incomplete without rental real estate. It is always good to start with single family, duplex, triplex or fourplex. Starting off by collecting multiple rental incomes increases the cash flow significantly while still yielding to all the other benefits mentioned above. The equity will also grow faster-allowing access to more capital for expansion into bigger units. Even when the economy is not as strong, people will still need a place to stay so the demand would be stable.

Paper asset investment should not be overlooked. As with other investment, research must be conducted to identify the best paper assets to buy. Getting in early is also very important as the value can become too diluted for any real significant gains if the company later lack innovation. Profitable paper assets such as stocks produces dividends which can be re-deposited into buying more stocks or simply cashed out.

There is no one size fits all when it comes to the type of online, offline, real estate or paper asset investment in particular. It should be something you know and understand. It should be profitable and always use arbitrage, when deciding what type of business to start or acquire.

CHAPTER TWO

Establish & Maintain Great Credit

Having great credit and knowing how to properly use it is financial literacy most basic principle

The World Operates on Debt and so Should You

Almost everything we do nowadays is predicated on credit. When you need to borrow money, rent an apartment or even apply for certain jobs, expect to be asked to sign a consent form for credit inquiry. The world is funded by the world central banks who has the authority to print money and issue credit. Governments and kings utilize debt from these banks to advance their causes and capital growth. To get access to this funds, they must be creditworthy and follow terms of the funding. Like nations, when capital is needed, people also tend to banks, usually a lesser and local bank. When individuals or corporations don't have the funds needed or choose not to use their own money, they seek to borrow it. The monetary system operates on credit and debt so knowing how to use it to your advantage is fundamental.

While family members or friends may be able to lend you money, most will not if you don't appear to be financially responsible. The yardstick used to measure whether you'll pay back the money is your past habits of paying other bills. Other indications are how you manage money in terms of your debt to income ratio and whether you have an income producing job or business. Great credit can take you much further in life and in business especially when you are in pursuit of wealth.

If your family and friends consider the above factors to determine if they should lend you money, they have done what all financial institution do as a minimum pre-qualification for lending. Knowing that all banks will go through a series of checklist before agreeing to give you capital, it would be a wise not to apply unless you can meet all the requirements necessary to secure the money. The fact that you know what to expect is great but securing funding for your business is greater, in fact, a key recipe for building wealth. As you will see in later chapters, using borrowed money for business and investments will help you accelerate your goals.

Use Debt or Other People Money (OPM)

Just think if you can start a lucrative business with a moderate or substantial startup cost and do it using the bank's money. Ladies and gentleman, when you secure a loan, you're in fact using other people's money. To qualify for this promissory note, you'll have to demonstrate a sound credit history, some collateral, an income and a few less significant things such as experience, insurance, and comprehensive business plan. This chapter will cover what preparations should be done in establishing and maintaining great credit before you apply for a business loan.

After you have earned cash, either on your own or through a series of avenues covered in chapter one, it's time to establish credit. Credit is obtained when goods or services are rendered with expectation of a later payment. It is predicated on trust and it is essential that every person and institution build it. I cannot overemphasize the importance of establishing great credit. Doing so will enable you secure low interest loans or lines of credit for your business startup, maintenance, expansion and other investments. Of course there are other ways to secure funding however this chapter will focus on credit as it makes life much easier in terms of tapping into an easy resource of other people's money.

The three main national credit reporting agency in the United States of America are Equifax, Trans Union, and Experian. These agencies have a large database of everyone's credit history supplied by creditors and makes it accessible to anyone with permission to inquire. They also have a host of services to help you monitor and protect your credit at all times. Although these services are not needed for the beginner, it should be of interest to you once you have establish great credit. All things that have substantial value should be protected. With identity theft and its derivatives on the rise, I employ you to take measures to protect your great credit when you reach that status. You will use it over and over again as leverage to secure assets as your net worth continues to ascend.

Steps for Establishing Credit

Establishing credit requires a few basic steps. First, you must show a history of paying as agreed. If you do not have a credit history, you may start one by applying for an initial credit card from a local credit union or bank. If you are denied due to lack of credit, you'll have to apply for a secure credit card. This simply means you will have to pay a deposit. Use the card minimally and always make your monthly payments on time. I repeat, never make late payments as it will defeat the purpose. It takes about six months for your credit status to be reported to the three agencies mentioned above. You can take back your deposit and apply for an unsecured credit card after your initial credit has been established.

Most initial cards will have five hundred dollars limit and this amount will increase over time as you continue to make timely monthly payments as indicated on your statements. Having a combination of a bank loan and credit card will produce the best results as one is considered fixed and the other, revolving. In cases where the initial loan is denied, you can apply for a credit builder loan as well. This alternative method will allow you to deposit your money into your savings account and your bank or credit union will regard it as a loan. Again for starters, a good amount would be just five hundred dollars. They are in essence helping you establish credit by forcing you to save throughout the term or as agreed. If you have enough money to spare for let's say six months, you may elect to do both unsecured credit card as well as credit builder loan simultaneously.

Remember the intended purpose and only use the money for necessities. It is of grave importance to remain discipline with your credit building activities. The loan is basically locked in for 6 months so you cannot use that money. The credit card, however, can be used but make sure to never reach the credit limit at any monthly statement period before re-payments are made. For maximum effectiveness, on five hundred dollars credit limit, do not exceed two hundred and fifty dollars in usage any giving month unless you intend on paying the entire balance each month before the statement date. This is the date that your balance is documented and your credit card utilization is reported to the credit reporting agencies. As long as you maintain low utilization of less than thirty percent of your account limit, paying by the due date is fine. Again, pay close attention the two dates mentioned above. Statement date captures your balance at the time statement is printed while due date requires at least a minimum payment. Statement date precedes due date by three to four weeks.

Devise Wealth Credit Bureau Scorecard

Characteristic	Attribute	Possible Points	Points Received
Age of Tradelines	0-1 Year 1-2 Year 3-4 Year 5 Years or More	60 90 120 180	180
Number of Tradelines	1 2 3 4 5 6 7	70 80 90 80 70 60 50	90
Number of Accounts Delinquent in Last Year	0 1 2 3 4 or More	150 75 50 25 10	150
Number of Accounts Greater than 90 Days Delinquent in 24 Months	0 1 2 3 4 or More	100 75 60 60 25	100
% of Open Accounts Never Delinquent	100-90 50-80 25-49 0-24	100 75 50 15	100
Number of Bank Cards	0 1 2 3 4 5 6 7 or More	10 20 30 50 70 60 50 20	70
Number of Bank Cards where Balance is at least 30% of the Credit Limit	0 1 2 3 4 5 6 or More	100 75 65 55 50 30 10	100
Number of Inquiries in the Last Six Months	1 2 3 4 5 or More	60 50 40 30 20	60
Totals			850

The scorecard above is in an example of the metrics used by the credit bureaus to determine credit score. It is based on the points system. The first item is the age of trade lines. A trade line is simply a record of all activity of credit extended to a borrower and reported to a credit bureau. You can achieve the maximum points of 180 when you have reached 5 years or more of credit activity. To reach the peak points of 90, the number of trade lines, you must maintain is 3. Any more or less will cause a reduction in points. A maximum points of 150 is automatically given is there are no delinquent activity within one year. Bear in mind that 4 or more delinquent activity will cause you to lose almost the entire 150 points. Another 100 points is awarded if the number of accounts delinquent is greater than ninety days within the last twenty four months is zero. However, four or more cases of this will cause you to lose almost the entire 100 points. When ninety to one hundred percent of your open accounts are never delinquent, you get another 100 points but if only twenty four percent or less meets this criteria, you'll lose almost the entire 100 points. The peak points of 70 can be attained with a total of four bank cards. Any more or less diminished points in that regards. When the number of bank cards where the balance is at least thirty percent is zero, you'll score the full 100 points while six or more bank cards with at least thirty percent balance would result in a drastic drop to almost 0 points. One or less inquiries in the last six months will get you all 60 points however five or more will bring you to a floor level of almost 0 points. The total number of points is 850 and it can be achieved when this metrics is properly understood and followed.

A credit card is a very helpful tool for building great credit, nevertheless if used improperly, it can cost you lots of money in interest and hurt your credit history a great deal. It is worth noting that no interest is charged when balances are paid in full each month. This is different from the minimum payment required. When using the credit card as a tool to build great credit, its okay to pay the minimum required as long as it's paid on time every month. You will pay very high interest when you choose this route so if it's possible, pay the complete balance each month and never worry about interest.

Upon completion of the terms and timely payments, you'll now have a loan payment on your credit history as the credit union or bank will report your credit history to the three reporting agencies. Consequently, you may now retrieve the deposit you were forced to save. Any additional loan or credit card request should be approved without a deposit and you're on your way to establishing great credit as long as you continue to pay on time.

First compare important benefits from at least 2 banks such as interest rate, cash back rewards, credit limit and fraud protection. Making monthly payments on time, never maxing your credit limit, and using it for necessities only are important factors to remember. When you have completed the first 6 months of secure credit card and loan payments, withdrawn your deposit and have received an unsecured card and loan, follow the same good practice of discipline.

Those that opt out of secure loans and credit card can either find a co-signer or become an authorized user on someone else card. Perhaps a family member or a good friend with good credit can help. It will work the same way in building your credit when the cards are used and repayments are made on time per terms of agreement. A word of caution, please don't disappoint anyone who put their credit on the line by co-signing for you or adding you as an authorized user. Either of these methods or both will be sufficient after six months for you to get your own initial secure credit card and loan.

To check your credit after the first 6 months and free yearly report thereafter, simply visit annualcreditreport.com and you'll get it for free. The report does not include a FICO score that lenders use to determine risk however it is safe to assume its good if your credit score itself is good due to timely payments of debt. To be sure, however, you can order the FICO score directly from Equifax, Experian, or Trans Union.

Devise Wealth Credit Bureau Scorecard Pie Chart Example

- Age of Tradelines
- # of Tradelines
- # of Accounts Delinquent in Last Year
- # of Accounts Greater than 90 Days Delinquent in 24 Months
- % of Open Accounts Never Delinquent
- # of Bank Cards
- # of Bank Cards where Balance is at least 30% of the Credit Limit
- # of Inquiries in the Last Six Months

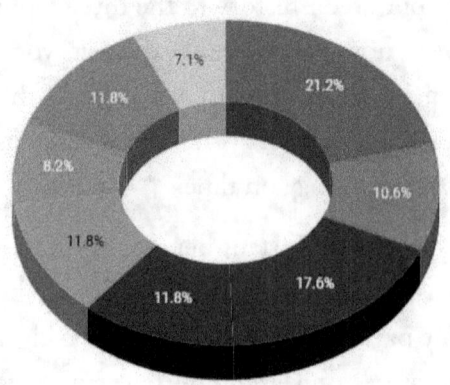

Based on the scorecard table example, this pie chart illustrated criteria for points and its equivalent percentages. For instance, the age of tradelines has the highest number of points, consequently the highest percentage of 21.2. The number two spot at 17.2 percent belongs to the number of accounts delinquent in the last year. To be perfectly clear, keep it at zero to enjoy the maximum percentage. For the next three criteria, the maximum percentage of 11.8 respectively can be attained. They are when the number of accounts greater than ninety days delinquent in twenty four months is zero, percentage of open accounts never delinquent is 100, and the number of bank cards where the balance is at least thirty percent of the credit limit is zero.

After a year of establishing your credit, which should be excellent if you've followed the process outlined above, with a qualified income, your next step if you don't already have it, is to apply for a home loan. Having a history of timely mortgage payments along with the revolving payments of a credit card will catapult you into a prospective business loan candidate. This is especially true when you have made mortgage payments for several years because you now have equity in your home.

This equity will also be used later to secure more investments in yet another wealth strategy.

What is being conveyed here is that unless you have the capital necessary to start a lucrative business, you have to borrow it. The banks and other savvy investors will not lend the money unless you demonstrate a few things. Among them are income, sound credit history, collateral such as a home or other equity, and life insurance in case of a tragic death before the principal and interest of the loan is paid in its entirety. No one likes to lend money without being certain that they will get it back.

Even if you have the capital, it is not advisable to use your own money to start a business. If you have the money but have not established your credit, you should do so right away. Doing it will afford you the discipline needed so that your money is used the right way. Being financially literate in today's world is incomplete without mastering credit and the use of it. The notion that you will excel in business without credit is unwise and should be reconsidered.

For those that may have no credit or impaired credit, but have the capital to start a business, go ahead and proceed. Make sure that you begin the process of repairing or establishing your credit simultaneously with the start of your business. Again, this age demands the use of debit and credit as even United Stated of America, the biggest corporation in the world uses this method in managing its affairs of taxes, military, social security, Medicare, subsidies, payroll, capital growth and other responsibilities. Furthermore, you will cringe when you discover in a later chapter what your money could have done if you had leveraged it by borrowing instead of using your own money. There are no incentives for using your own money and it should be avoided whenever possible. With that said, lenders typically will require a little down payment usually ten to twenty-five percent depending on the investment. Be that as it may, even seventy-five percent of let's say one hundred thousand dollars in borrowed money is seventy-five thousand dollars of other people's money that can be used to further your investment aspirations. It will become clearer if it hasn't already that, there is no substitute for establishing great credit if you intend to be rich.

Repairing your credit takes time, effort and payments. Old debts can be negotiated with the owner of the debt as most lenders usually sell the debt after some time. When negotiating a debt, be sure to have everything in writing. Make an offer to begin the process and once an agreement has been reached. Do all you can to meet your end of the agreement. There are many cases where the debt would be reduced significantly and adjustments made in reporting, when the agreement is reached and payments are made on time.

All Debt Are Not Equal

It is a huge misconception that people with money will continue to have money. The fact remains that your money will take care of you if you manage it properly. How many times have you heard the story of rich people who lost all their fortune? It happens all the time yet a fairly large portion of people do not learn from it. It is not difficult if you remain in charge of your finances. Everyone should have a clear understanding of the genius of compound interest and make it work for you at all cost. I will say it again; anyone who makes compound interest work for them has entered a great path for accelerated growth. Think about it for a second. Isn't that what all the banks and financial institutions have done? We can all see how well off they are.

Without attempting to teach compound interest, here's what you need to know. It is a mathematical calculation that is based on compounding every interest earned into the principle as it is earned and on top of the accumulated interest. It grows very quickly over time. When you borrow, you'll pay compound interest but lend and you'll be on the receiving end of the compound interest. We will dig deeper into the lending strategy when we discuss asset classes.

A thirty-year mortgage of one hundred thousand dollars at five percent interest is around one hundred and ninety-five thousand and over a quarter million dollars with taxes and insurance. Why not put that money to work for yourself instead of giving it all to the lender. You can counter compound interest by paying the thirty-year mortgage in five to seven years using one of the simple techniques I've illustrated below. With this, your house will be completely paid off so you own the entire equity and you would have freed up the monthly mortgage payment so you can buy more money making assets.

Just a bit of financial literacy will suggest that money should never be idle. The equity is like money just sitting around so alternatively that equity would be used to make additional asset acquisitions. The consequence will be more equity and more cash flow. I promise we will re-visit this great wealth opportunity later when we cover leverage. For now, our focus is to eliminate debt and become bad debt free. Please note that I said bad debt free. When you decide to build wealth, your focus should be to only buy assets. Anything that makes you money is an asset. Every effort should be made to avoid things that cost money but doesn't yield any money. Those things create bad debt and if you have some, eliminate it. Here are three simple aspects that cannot be overlooked when it comes to money management. The primary aspect that cannot be ignored is becoming bad debt free. Please understand that debt can be used in a magnificent way but bad debt has no place in wealth building. When one is able to clearly differentiate between the two, looking back leaves a sense of regret of how much waste has taken place. It does none the less motivate, with sticking to the process of eliminating bad debt forever.

When one makes a decision to be bad debt free, he or she must make a commitment and stick to it. No matter how gigantic your bad debts are, it can be overturned if you follow these few simple rules. First, let's define bad debt so that we'll all be on the same page. Bad debt in its simplest term is money you've borrowed that does not make you money. Necessary recurring bills are not classified as debt at all, although they should be monitored to avoid waste. It is for this simple reason that recurring bills such as insurance and utilities will always be paid with no end in sight. Loans however always have a payoff date so if it doesn't produce cash flow, let's eliminate it.

Basic Bad Debt Elimination Step One

Take inventory of all your debt with total amounts owed, monthly minimum required, interest rate and payoff date. Proceed to add all your other bills such as utilities, insurances, food, gas etc. Please note that bills may not have an amount owed, interest rate or payoff date as it is recurrent in nature. It is very necessary to do this exercise because subsequent rules are dependent on this first step. It's like traveling to an unfamiliar territory with a starting point on some sort of navigation system or map. Proceed to arrange your debt from smallest to largest. Re-arrange the previous list again from the largest interest rates to the smallest. The table below serves as an example:

Devise Wealth Debt Elimination Inventory Example

Debt	Owed	Monthly	Interest Rate	Payoff Date
Credit Card	3,000	50	22%	6/2018
Car Loan	18,000	500	9%	3/2019

Mortgage	120,000	950	6%	12/2030
Electricity		200		
Water		50		
Phone		50		
Gas		200		
Food		500		
Car Insurance		100		
Health Insurance		200		
Emergency/ Misc		100		

The above is just an example. Create your own table based on the example above. You are now ready to take steps toward eradicating these debts, but first, calculate your total net earnings per month. If your total earnings per month is less than your total monthly required obligation, you must do some radical changes. You can either eliminate some of your unnecessary bills or get a supplemental job. While the numbers may discourage you depending on your situation, you will be glad to know that once you start this process, it becomes easier as you see your debt disappearing before your eyes.

Basic Bad Debt Elimination Step Two

Pay the very minimum monthly requirement of everything on your list except the top debt on your list. Again bear in mind that I said everything except your single top debt. For the top debt item, pay the minimum required plus a maximum addition that you can afford. If you cannot pay anything higher than the minimum on the top debt item, there is a waste somewhere. Find where you're wasting money and stop it, then use it to pay extra on the top debt. If you try and cannot identify any waste, then taking part-time or odd jobs to earn extra money for this purpose is a good initiative.

Do you see where I'm going? Keep reading because you will soon. After meeting the bare minimum of all your other bills, you'll now pay as much as you can stand towards the top debt on your chart. Even just $100 more will make a noticeable difference, however, I do encourage you to pay as much as possible. Continue to pay in that fashion until top debt number one is completely eliminated. Be sure to specify any extra payments towards your car loan or mortgage as principal only. This will further eliminate more unnecessary interest.

As soon as the top debt is eradicated, the second top debt now becomes the top debt. Proceed to apply the same method except add the entire payment amount that you were paying on the previous debt towards the second debt. When the second debt is totally paid, apply the entire payment amount from the two previous debt towards the third debt. Continue this path until every debt has vanished. You should be delighted as you've done something that many people either don't know or are not willing to do.

You have now discovered how to protect yourself from the negative effects of compound interest. I mean the banks and other financial institutions are not very happy with me because I have revealed several of their greatest secrets thus far. They give loans for an extended time and charge interest but they fail to mention compound interest. Consequently, borrowers end up paying way too much with respect to what they borrowed. The longer you take to pay your debt, the more interest you pay.

I'm going to help you put an end to that nonsense. In fact, you'll know exactly how long it will take for you to become debt free based on your unique situation and calculations. The system I'm teaching you is very effective and it does much more than eliminate debt. We'll cover all the other benefits in the next few sections.

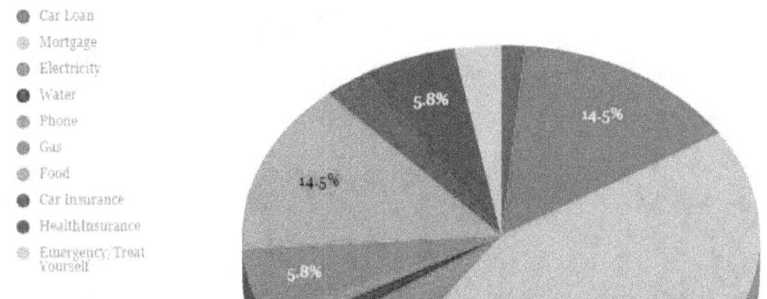

* Percentage is based on the total amount of debt and bills found in the Debt/Bills Inventory Table

This debt/bills elimination pie chart example was created directly from the example illustrated previously from the debt/bills inventory table. As you can see, the mortgage is the biggest liability. It has 43.5% debt and it therefore takes the top spot. Next, the highest ones belongs to car loan and food. They are both at 14.5% each. The third is a three way tie among electricity, health insurance and gas. These three are all at

5.8% each. The next one is the emergency/treat yourself fund and it is at 2.9%. The remaining four are less significant, however they are important as well. They make up less than 2.9% and they are water, phone credit card and car insurance. Of those four, credit card is an actual debt so it can be completely eliminated. The other three are bills, therefore they will continue to re-occur for as long as you exist.

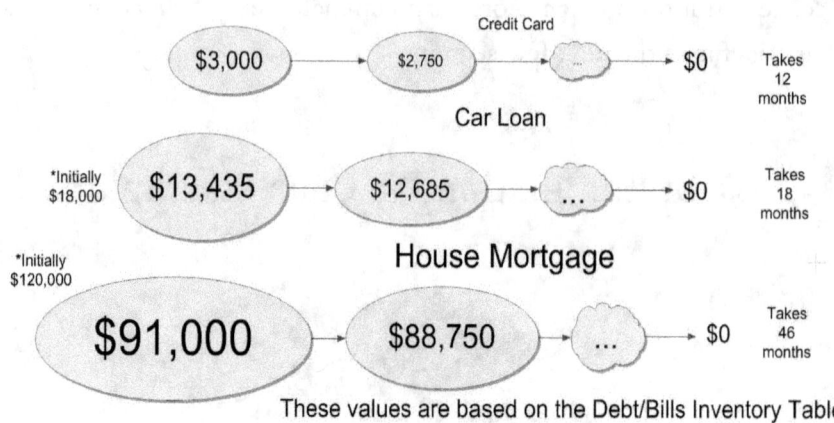

This flow chart example is also based on the previous debt/bills inventory table example. With only two hundred dollars a month in extra payment, you will be completely out of debt in just under 7 years. You are looking at a total of around 76 months. Let me explain. You are going to start off by paying the credit card debt. Simply apply the extra two hundred dollars to the fifty dollars minimum payment for a total of two hundred fifty dollars a month. In 12 months exactly, your credit card debt will be completely eliminated.

You will then take the entire balance that was being applied to the credit card towards the next debt. In this case, it will be your car loan. Keep in mind that during the 12 months, your minimum payment was was on the car loan so the balanced was reduced from eighteen thousand dollars to thirteen thousand four hundred and thirty five dollars. This amount has the interest already factored in. This new balance on the car loan will take eighteen months to eliminate with a payment of seven hundred and fifty dollars. That is the minimum payment of five hundred dollars you were already making plus the two hundred and fifty dollars you just freed up when the credit card bill was eliminated.

Don't stop, proceed full speed and apply that extra seven hundred and fifty dollars that's now available from the car loan payments to your next debt. In our example, it is the mortgage. So far you have eliminated two debt and it took a total of 30 months. During that time, your mortgage was still being paid at a minimum of one thousand five hundred dollars a month. Factor in interest and you would have paid twenty nine thousand dollars. Subtract it from the one hundred twenty thousand dollars and your new balance will be ninety one thousand dollars.

At the new balance, all you have to do is add the minimum payment to the extra payment which now becomes two thousand two hundred and fifty dollars a month towards your mortgage each month. If you do this, your mortgage will be completely eliminated in 46 months or 3.8 years. So in under 7 years, you have managed to get yourself completely out of debt based on the figures in this example. You now have no debt and all you did was apply an extra two hundred dollars towards your debt every month and kept going. Imagine what you can do with two thousand two hundred and fifty dollars extra money, do debt, and all bills and expenses paid. Building wealth is now at your fingertips.

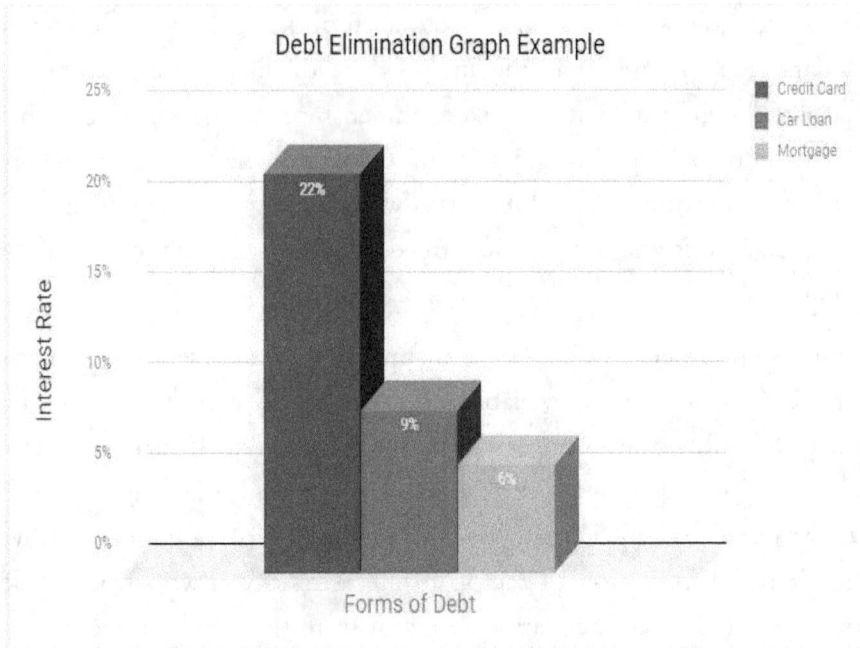

*Interest values based on the total amount of debt and bills found in the Debt/Bills Inventory Table

This debt elimination graph example is based on the previous debt/bills inventory table but this time, we are only focusing on debt, not bills. You have three main debt as illustrated on the graph. The first one is highest interest rate debt and it is the credit card debt. It has an interest rate of 22%. If you look at the previous example, you can see that the credit card debt was eliminated in 12 months. The next debt is the car loan with an interest rate of 9% and it was eliminated in 18 months. The first two debt have been eliminated in just 30 months. Now the last debt which is the mortgage takes a little longer however with the money from the first two debts, you are looking at 46 months and the mortgage is completely paid off. The mortgage debt has an interest rate of 6%. In just 76 months, all three debts have been completed eliminated based on just an extra two hundred dollars a month payment. Do you realize how powerful this basic system is in terms of not only paying off debt but using the same method to build wealth? You will as you keep reading.

Debt Elimination Checklist Example

- ❏ Create a table like the Debt/Bills Inventory Table example illustrated
- ❏ List all your debts from lowest to highest interest rate
- ❏ Next reorganize the interest rates from highest to lowest
- ❏ Pay monthly minimum on every debt on the list except for the single top debt
- ❏ For the top debt, pay minimum required and maximum addition you can afford
- ❏ Continue steps 1 through 5 until top debt is completely eliminated
- ❏ As soon as top debt is eliminated, the second highest interest debt becomes the top debt, add all the extra payment from the previous debt towards the new top debt
- ❏ Be sure to specify all extra payments towards the loan and mortgage as "principal only" payment
- ❏ As soon as second debt is eliminated, third highest interest debt becomes the new top debt, add all the extra payment from the previous debt towards the new top debt
- ❏ Continue this path until all debt are completely eliminated

This checklist is a quick guide to help you quickly create a plan for debt elimination. Remember all that was accomplished with just $200 extra payment a month in terms of debt elimination. Much more wonderful things can be done in terms of building wealth with that same extra money. I hope you have now realized that building wealth is doable. Let this serve as part of the motivation as read on.

Post Debt Elimination Plan

Once you've rectified your bad debt problems, you should do everything within your capacity to remain bad debt free. A few positive changes will take shape during the process of bad debt elimination. First, bad debt will begin to shrink as your credit score increases. A tremendous amount of interest will be avoided as this system works outside the realm of the paralyzing effect of compound interest. More cash flow is produced for the next acquisition of assets. As you can clearly see, more funds are now available therefore you could also begin to pay for personal things without taking a loan. The ability to do this for the first time is sure to bring great joy to your heart. Rightfully so, after all, you've worked hard to arrive at this point in your life.

It is advisable to take it a step further after all the debts been paid and continue putting money away as if the debts still exist. People who do this find themselves building short term savings at an astronomical rate. It's truly a beautiful thing to see. As I told you, your money will take care of you if you take care of your money. For starters, money accumulated must be used to buy more assets, a concept that I will continue to push since it is key to becoming rich. It is my primary declaration that any debt that yields a substantial margin is a good debt. Although your land and home appreciate in value, it should be paid off in its' entirety.

When this happens, it opens new doors of opportunities that can be a game changer. Larger sums of loan needed to start a business that can create a fortune are now within reach. You see, lenders look at key factors for determining eligibility such as business plan, credit history, credit limit, debt to income ratio, net worth, and collateral. At this point, your profile is ripe for a loan more than an overwhelming amount of candidates. With some research, you'll be bombarded with so many businesses that can make you very rich in a short time. The key is to perform due diligence along with your team.

Accelerated Mortgage Payment

Please understand that taking thirty years to pay off your mortgage is not a wise thing and it can impede one's quest for becoming rich. With a simple but disciplined method, anyone that qualifies for a home loan can pay off their house in five to seven years and get on with the business of building wealth. The look on everyone's faces whenever I show them this method is priceless. Although this information is not magic or unethical, the banks would prefer if you were not in the knowing.

These banks are in business for profits and they intend to continue raking in large sums of money from consumers' ignorance and ill-informed decisions. Very often, banks make attempts to get folks to re-finance after they've paid for several years. What they fail to tell you is that every time a homeowner re-finances, the clock starts all over again. That means you are going to pay more interest than before. You see, when you take out a mortgage loan for thirty years, most of your monthly payment goes towards your interest until the 17th year. Imagine being contacted after seventeen years of payment with a lower interest bait offer. Most people hear lower interest and they fall for it. Don't be the one that these banks take advantage of with their manipulations. The table below illustrates how your money is applied towards a 30-year loan of one hundred thousand dollars at 5 percent fixed interest.

Devise Wealth System Amortization Table Example

Year	Principle	Interest	Loan Balance
2018	$851.66	$2,906.08	$99,148.34
2020	$1,596.63	$4,845.21	$96,032.79
2022	$1,764.20	$4,677.64	$92,590.27
2024	$1,949.31	$4,492.53	$88,786.50
2026	$2,153.88	$4,287.96	$84,583.58
2028	$2,379.90	$4,061.94	$79,939.59
2030	$2,629.65	$3,812.19	$74,808.24
2032	$2,905.63	$3,536.21	$69,138.41
2034	$3,210.53	$3,231.31	$62,873.60
2036	$3,547.45	$2,894.39	$55,951.34
2038	$3,919.73	$2,522.11	$48,302.66
2040	$4,331.08	$2,110.76	$39,851.29
2042	$4,785.58	$1,656.26	$30,513.05
2044	$5,287.80	$1,154.04	$20,194.83
2046	$5,842.70	$599.14	$8,793.81
2048	$2,652.17	$33.25	$0.00

In mathematics, there are many ways and formulas to solving a problem but there is only one correct answer. The one correct answer for mortgage as it pertains to wealth building is quick payoff. Let the information covered here serve to motivate you in paying off your mortgage swiftly. It is not easy but it is smart. It puts you in a position to stop handing over money that should be making you rich. Use any of the methods that I'm disclosing because the end is always the same, accelerated mortgage payment.

If you own a home, simply apply for a home equity line of credit or HELOC. Deposit all your earnings into this account and pay all your bills from the account. Make sure that your total earnings is greater than your total debt and bills by at least twenty percent. Pay your necessary monthly recurring bills such as utilities, grocery, gas, fun money, and others as usual from this account. Proceed to pay the minimum on all debt except the lowest debt from a loan or credit card. Apply the remainder of HELOC balance towards the lowest loan or credit card debt. Apply money left over due to low balance of the lowest loan or credit card to the next lowest debt. Repeat the process until all the HELOC has been exhausted and many debts eradicated. You'll more than like have only a small portion of mortgage and HELOC as the two debts remaining. Don't rest, immediately target the mortgage balance and apply the extra money that you've just freed up from all your previous debts towards the mortgage while paying the minimum on the HELOC. The result should be overwhelming and therefore the payoff will become even faster.

Give your lender instructions to apply all extra payment over the minimum payment to principal only. Continue and watch your principal disintegrate. Finally, when the mortgage is paid in full, apply all the extra money towards the HELOC. This method or a variation of it will not only produce accelerated mortgage payment but get you completely out of debt. Before long, you are totally debt free and can quickly convert all the payment amount into wealth building assets. The lack of financial education is the blame for people taking 30 years to pay off their mortgage. Learn about finances and use the information to keep your money for wealth building instead of enriching the banks.

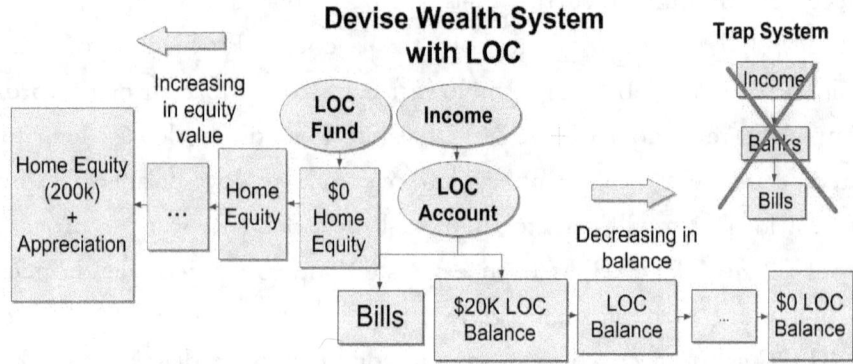

These figures are not typical for anyone in particular. It is an example to illustrate my point.

Simple Method for Very Good Credit

Here is yet another example to eliminate bad debt, increase credit limit, and raise your credit score substantially. Simply apply for two credit cards with no interest balance transfer. This time, the entire inventory of your bills illustrated in the previous section will be paid directly with the credit cards. Use your credit cards to pay monthly car loan, mortgage, electricity, water, phone, gas, food, car insurance, health insurance and emergency/treat yourself allowance. Pay the entire amount on the credit cards monthly statements on time but make sure your credit card balance is less than thirty percent of your credit limit by statement date. When the entire balance is paid by the due date, you've just made room to use the cards again as credit cards are revolving.

In just 6 months, you're going to get a credit limit increase as well and an increase in credit score. Follow the same practice and enjoy another increase every six months. This simple method will make a very noticeable difference in just a few 6 months cycle in terms of credit limit and credit score increase. As always, the mortgage or other loan should be paid with additional payment towards the principal only. The main differences among the basic bad debt elimination, the accelerated mortgage payment and the simple method are that bills are paid directly from your checking account, HELOC account and credit card account respectively.

Standard Method for Near Perfect Credit

Now that you get the idea, let's take a look at the standard method. Assuming the bills remain the same as the table in the previous section. Go ahead and apply for a line of credit. Deposit your entire paycheck into the line of credit account. Pay all your bills directly from the line of credit account. The key to this method is paying the minimum on all the bills and apply all the extra money towards principal only for the car payment. As soon as the car loan has been completely paid off, use all the extra money towards the principal only on the mortgage. Again, you'll begin to see credit line increasing, accelerated debt elimination, credit score increase and debt free account within a short time. You must have decent credit history to qualify for a credit cards, lines of credit and HLOC for that matter.

Standard Method 2.0

When you combine the simple method with the standard, you now have an even faster credit solution with larger increase and a perfect credit score as well as debt elimination. This way of using credit is preferred. It yields the biggest rewards. Simply conditioning yourself to this way of thinking and your entire journey will begin to move much smoother than other alternatives. One must be very disciplined because if these payments are not made on time, the impact will be negative and therefore will defeat the purpose and cause setbacks.

A couple with a household income of just sixty thousand dollars and the same bills illustrated above can be totally free of debt in just under five years with this method and move into the top ten percent in credit score. Being in this position of having one hundred percent equity, top credit score, large home equity, line of credit, large credit cards limit as well as cash flow of about four thousand dollars after taxes, you've positioned yourself for securing a substantial business loan without a problem.

The average lifespan of humans is 80 years. The first 22 of those years are just for school for the most part. That is if you opt out of specializing. Those that further, their training could tag on another three to seven years depending on the area of study. Most people after school have been thoroughly indoctrinated to get a job and become an employee. If and when you finally realize that may be the wrong way to proceed, you may very well be thirty years old. The agenda to become rich now lingers but you are close to half of your life's expectancy. You cannot afford to wait another thirty years before starting the wealth creation process. Start it now and do it quickly so in 5 years, you are totally free of debt.

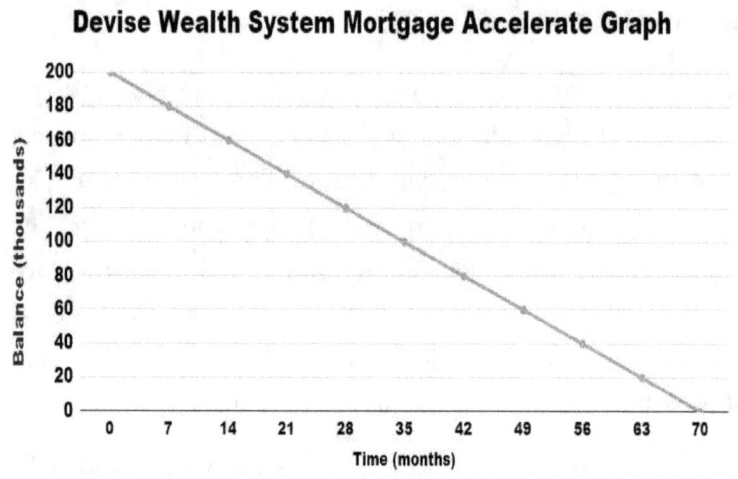

These figures are not typical for anyone in particular. It is an example to illustrate my point.

Do not ever wait to enjoy life. Take a great pleasure in life on the road to becoming rich. This means take care of your business while remembering to treat yourself well. When you begin to put wealth systems into place, you'll feel free when you indulge because you know there's more where that came from. Just having money without systems could never produce the same results.

Taking your newly found established resources such as cash flow, equity, great credit and leveraging them will begin what can potentially become generational wealth if you stick to the plan. Such standard method is only standard and should not be difficult at all when you are determined. The one thing that must be done to get the ball rolling is making the decision.

Benefits of Having Credit Cards

Contrary to the belief of many, credit cards have benefits that are enjoyed by financially literate and responsible people. For instance, with the knowledge of credit cards types, terms, and benefits, you can acquire these cards strategically and enjoy perks such as cash back rewards among others. Many also enjoy accumulated points for free travel and hotel in addition to their cash back rewards. If carefully done, one could take a vacation every single year for free. Imagine an excursion for a week or two each year and pay nothing all because you educated yourself and secured the correct cards and followed its terms. Not bad for using a card to conduct transactions that are necessary anyway and reaping rewards.

If you are disciplined, using credit cards to pay your bills will be much more viable than doing it from your checking account. It's not for everyone especially if you tend to be late on the payments that you already have. In that case, you'll dig yourself deeper into a hole. The benefits of credit card are to be enjoyed by individuals who are knowledgeable about them. These people tend to have the money already in place but then uses the card as a strategy for its security and to gain perks that could amount to free vacation flight, hotel, rental and meals once a year. No matter how much money you make from your wealth systems, strategic perks like these are always a thrill.

Having credit cards and using them responsibly also automatically raises your credit score and credit limit. The results are great credit and access to more credit. Of course, both of these benefits will help you in expanding your wealth system. It is also very convenient to use credit cards as opposed to cash. The risk is at a minimal compared to when carrying a large amount of cash. When there's a case of fraud or theft, most credit card companies will investigate and activate the fraud protection plan that most cards offer.

Credit card, most times, have no geographical barriers. If you move through several countries in Africa, Asia, or South America, there are certain currency exchanges that must take place with cash. You do not have that problem with credit cards. Using some cards to purchase your flight for that matter will actually increase your flyer miles and get you at times an upgrade from economy to first class and an upgrade in the hotel from a room to a suite and beyond. There are other benefits as well but even with all these benefits, it would be in your best interest to only take on credit cards if you can manage it properly.

Credit Card Don'ts

Although there are many incentives accrued with the carefully selected credit cards, certain practices must be avoided to prevent future trouble. Among them are how and where the cards are used, when payments are made, how much is paid, who initiates a credit card increase, what types of cards and in what order are they acquired.

Never use a credit card to withdraw cash from an ATM because there are charges associated with it. Don't ignore creditors when they call about your bill. It is better to face it head on and resolve the issue. They have every incentive to work something out and collect the payment than to just report it to the credit bureaus. They will not hesitate however to do so because they know reporting it usually motivate people to finally make payment arrangements. Waiting until it is reported affects your credit score so stop it in its track. Even if you think a bill is not important, go ahead and pay or resolve it because if it is handed over to collections, they will report it if not resolved.

It is nice to get balance transfer offers that have no interest charges for an extended period of time. You must still maintain a low utilization so don't transfer all your cards onto just one unless you keep it at thirty percent or below. Creditors aren't very happy when they see utilization that's higher because they see it as risky. Conversely, you'll have a much higher score with low balances.

Due to the fact that staying under thirty percent is the rule of thumb, it is better to have a high credit limit. If you are not able to get an increase sufficient enough to stay under the mark, more credit cards may be a viable option. The way it is calculated is the sum of all the cards versus the utilization. As long as you maintain the thirty percent or below, you will not take a hit. Spread the usage so all the cards have lower utilization. Remember that more credit means lower interest rates for you.

I always tell people to pay off their balance in its entirety every month if feasible. When circumstances prevent you from doing so, pay at least the minimum. Never pay below the minimum due and of course never make a late payment. Paying below the minimum is regarded as not paying at all. Avoid this from occurring by setting reminders or picking payment dates that are easy for you to remember.

If you decide to use the multiple credit cards strategy to keep a lower utilization rate, do not open more than one credit card at a time. Not heeding to this advice will cause a credit score decrease as an inquiry is placed on your report. Space them out so you can maintain a decent average account age. Since the average age of all your trade lines are so important, don't ever close your oldest account when picking a new card, do your due diligence on them. Just picking a card without knowing the benefits, features and perks can get you in trouble. Some cards for example has annual fees. It is not always bad to go after a card with fees especially when it has a signing bonus, cash back rewards, flyer miles and other perks. Paying attention to cards for instance that has a foreign transaction fee for those that travel a lot is of great importance. Imagine having to pay three percent fee every time you use your card outside of your country.

Purchase and Pay Bills with Credit Cards

Instead of paying bills out of your checking account, people that understand what they stand to gain often elect to purchase and pay their bills with credit cards. A continued credit score increase or high credit score stability, increase in credit limits, and greater credit card reward offers are just a few of the reasons why people choose to transact with credit as opposed to their checking account.

It does make sense for responsible people to use their credit cards to pay bills as long as there are no fees associated with it. Do some research on your particular bills because some companies charge a fee each time a bill is paid with a credit card. If some of your bills fall into this category, you can separate them and only utilize your cards with the ones without a fee and pay the other bills using an alternative method.

Folks that pay bills with credit cards maximize their rewards and perks such as bonuses. Other than reaping the rewards of accrued points, it is convenient to pay bills with a credit card. You also get additional time to pay the credit card bill although this can be a trap for undisciplined users. What I like about this method is having the ability to track all your transactions on one statement. It is always good when you can bypass the process of writing checks and balancing your checkbook. When you decide to use your credit card to pay bills, be sure to follow the terms of the credit card.

Credit Cards on Steroids

Maximize your understanding of credit cards and you can use it to purchase assets. You read it right, gain great awareness of the credit card game and use it to fund certain businesses and real estate. For example business transactions that have a definite pay date would be a good candidate for credit card purchase. Another good one is real estate especially those that buy, fix and sell. These flippers can get it all done under six months in most cases. Well, the interest charged in six months is nothing compared to financing a house for fifteen to thirty years and having to pay so much to the lenders. Even better, credit card companies will offer you zero interest on transfers for up to one year.

Do you see how you could build an entire business with credit cards and not pay any interest? Of course, you do but I must caution you, do not take on such strategies unless you have a thorough understanding of all the terms as well as the venture that you intend to use it for. Remember that the credit card is just a tool. It cannot hurt you if you know how to properly use it. That said, you should not even entertain this idea if you are a rookie. This method is for people with a long great credit history and credit limit.

All the rules of credit cards still apply so it's not advisable for someone with a low credit limit to take on this strategy. The person however that has sufficient credit limit enough to purchase assets and stay under the thirty percent utilization rule has a lot to gain. Furthermore, such people are sophisticated businessmen or women and usually have experience with business credit. All the same, knowledgeable users can execute this method and later make the change from personal credit card to business credit card.

Business credit cards afford you the protection that personal credit card does not. When you have the correct structure for your business such as a corporation or an LLC, your business dealings are separate from your personal assets. In the event that the business defaults or fails to thrive, the credit company will take assets within your business only. That's a level of protection that does not exist for personal credit cards.

Although everyone goes into business to make money, the reality is that not everyone survives. Many as a result of not being knowledgeable about the industry that they are in, while others lack the systems necessary to succeed. To have that extra cushion of knowing that you can try without losing everything is a plus then if you fail it serves as a motivator in mitigating the risk. Surviving, however. Means being part of a fraternity of successful business people. Then, of course, there is the money which can be used to acquire more assets, therefore, making you richer.

What to Look for in Credit Cards

For starters, you will more than likely not qualified for the best cards but you can get there within a relatively short time. If you don't have any credit at all, start with a secured credit card. This simply means you'll have to pay a deposit which will be used as collateral for your credit line. Deposits are low and usually range between three hundred and five hundred dollars. Although you can charge up to the amount of the deposit but do not do it. Only charge up to thirty percent so you can keep a low utilization rate, a key factor that affects credit score.

At the end of your secure card term which is usually six months to a year, you will begin to get offers for regular unsecured cards. Take your time and compare offers. The best offers should have zero intro APR and low regular APR. Almost all the offers shouldn't have an annual fee but also look for zero interest on transfers and no transfer fees. There are times and situations when an annual fee makes sense. Select the card with rewards such as cash back and travel points and matching cash back. If you get a card or two that can do all the above, you have done your job. As a result of competition between the card companies, there are occasional promotions so be sure to really compare these cards for the best.

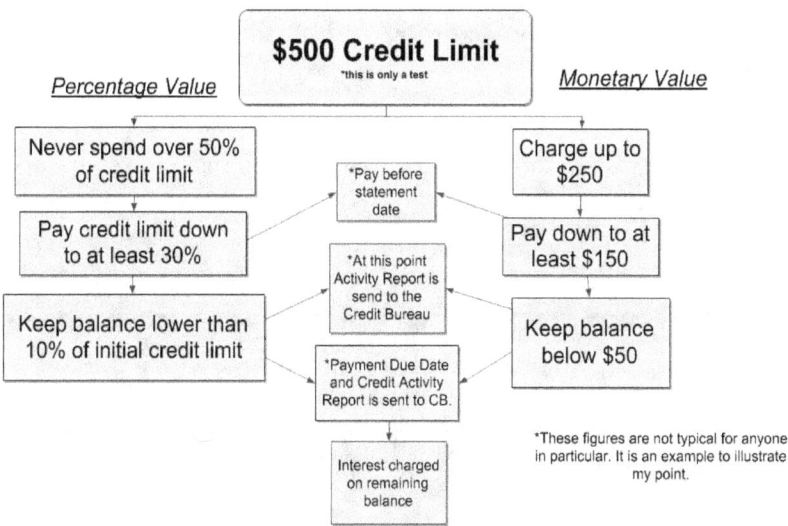

The most beneficial features to look for when shopping for credit cards are cash back rewards, travel rewards, and no annual fee respectively. Cash back is earned when you use the card to make purchases and is paid to you directly or issued as a credit on your account. Anyway, you can also redeem your points through gift cards, merchandise or travel. Although most cards offer one point per dollar, higher points can be earned for special categories such as the minimum amount of spending and certain merchants. Sign up bonuses has also become quite popular.

Some cardholders are offered double or triple points for groceries, gas, and travel. Many people will also enjoy extra points for using specific brands. Other benefits are extended return protection of up to ninety days as well as fraud and theft. Always look at the interest rates to make sure it's competitive. As I often say, don't get any card until you understand the terms and make sure you do not keep a monthly balance.

Knowing your spending habit will help you make the best credit card decision for the most benefits. A person that eats out a lot may target cards with points for dining and vice versa for travel. Do some calculations to make sure factors such as points per spending and annual fee if applicable all make sense for you. Know that it's about strategy therefore planning will ensure you get the most out of your credit cards. If you decide to use the strategy of churning which is basically getting more cards just for the rewards, make sure you do not spend more just to earn the perks.

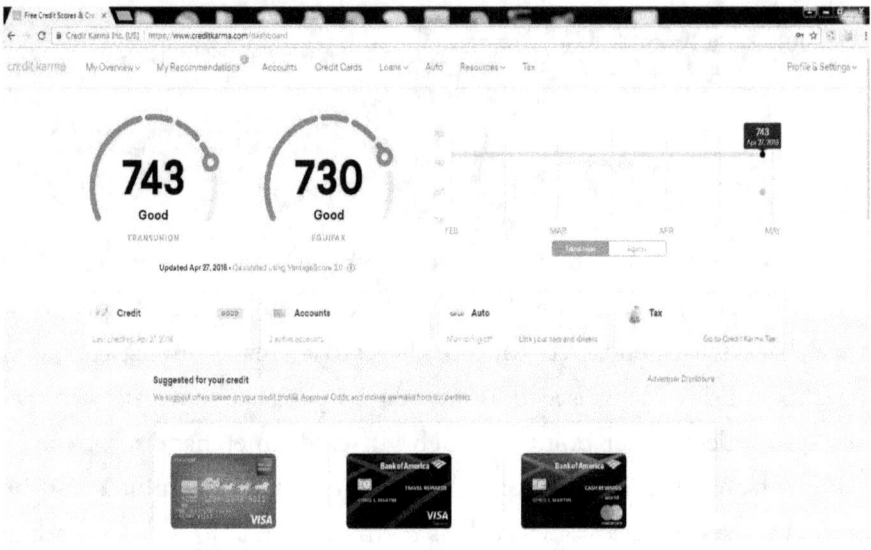

The credit score example above was retrieved just moments before the book went into publication. It belongs to one of my college students. This individual had no credit history at all when we devised a plan for her a little under a year ago. Now, she has a credit score of 743 from

Transunion, 730 points is scored by Equifax and at the time, Experian was late to the party, although their would be around the same numbers. The variations in credit score is caused by a multiple of factors. If the difference is significant, you may call the prospective credit bureau and ask them to explain. The method we used were the secure credit card and loan builder and it was done simultaneously. This is what she was able to accomplish. Notice that there are already credit card offers available to her and now she can apply for unsecured credit cards and loans. We are still working with her to get her into the 800 points line of great credit. By that time, she would be fully conditioned to maintain her great credit history. Again, it's all about financial education.

Financial Freedom Within Reach

One profitable business can literally make you wealthy and transform your net worth to a million dollars or more. When this inevitable outcome occurs, you'll be able to step it up another notch. You're now managing a million dollar portfolio and investment bankers are paying serious attention to you now. You've now met the minimum requirement to become an accredited investor so that securing a large loan to acquire larger assets is possible. Sophisticated investor will be covered in detail at a later chapter. Of course, you'll need a team if you decide to go through this route if you don't have one thus far. Your team at a minimum should consist of a business lawyer, an accountant, an investment banker, a secretary, staff, and a mentor in your field or industry. I intend to fill your brains with many business ideas.

If fifty people are asked to give their definition of financial freedom, everyone will say something different. What one man or woman considers being financially free may not come close to that of others. Be that as it may be, everyone should still pursue it. As I mentioned previously, it is a gratifying feeling when you reach what you define as financial freedom.

Some may say having a job that pays six figures is sufficient but in essence, that type of money can quickly disintegrate. There is absolutely nothing wrong with acquiring wealth or becoming forever rich ethically. The quest may not always be easy but the reward makes it all worth it. It is a beautiful ambition because you'll earn every bit of it the smart way and afford yourself, family, friends, and charity whatever financial requirement that comes your way. It is at that junction in your life that you can finally declare true financial freedom.

Chapter three is all about structuring your business in a manner that is consistent with longevity and success. It covers everything from the conception of a winning business idea, research, acquiring a building, proper setup, and much more. ROI, an important factor in determining whether to start a particular business or not will be covered. By the end of the chapter, you would be very familiar with all the steps necessary to open a business and begin serving customers.

CHAPTER THREE

Save Short Term Money for Assets

Structure your life as if it was a business and insert protective mechanism wherever necessary

Extra Money from a Job

It all starts with an idea. In the beginning, anyone with aspirations to become wealthy who does not poses it must secure initial capital. Capital is needed along with original or innovative ideas that create an opportunity to solve a problem for the masses. Such ideas developed from thoughts are often based on one's interest, passion or current environment. Meanwhile, the subject of capital can be acquired in many ways. Here's a multitude of quick and effective ways to generate the money required to get you started. It involves using your creativity to sell products, services or time of some sort.

You as a person are valuable, even if you don't have physical money in your hands or in the bank. Your time can earn you some money in the form of providing services. With this method, you are selling your time for a paycheck. You can get a job or a second job if needed to begin your journey of becoming and staying rich. You'll learn later in this book why having a job at the beginning may serve multiple purposes towards your goal. There's absolutely nothing wrong with it especially during the initial phase of your plan. At the right time, however, a shift will be made from being an employee to an employer, a key recipe.

For those who already have a job but spend all of their earnings on bills, a re-assessment has to be made. You may be living beyond your means. For an example, if you pay one thousand dollars for a smartphone, cash or installment, but have no money to invest in yourself, a shift in approach has to occur. A simple habitual change of buying unnecessary shiny object while on a quest to become rich is needed. That same money can buy an asset that will earn money over and over again. Another example maybe someone who drives a luxury vehicle with high monthly payments. At the end of the five or 6 years payment, the total could have been enough to make you rich. A house perhaps that is too big or cost too much should be downsized. Money is wasted on down payment, closing cost, mortgage, utilities, insurance, taxes, and maintenance among other things. My point is that you can find areas of waste, correct it, and use that money to buy assets. We will cover more on how acquiring assets makes you rich in a later chapter.

Tap into your Basic Skills & Talents

If you have a full-time job and getting a second job does not appeal to you, tap into your basic skills and talents. Anyone that can swim, sing, write, DJ, draw, paint, drive, dance, sew, cook, fight, walk or have other talents not mentioned here can sell their services in the form of lessons to earn extra cash. It is impossible for me to know everyone's talent and skill but look inside yourself and determine what you possess. Even walking a dog can generate extra cash as there are many busy middle class and wealthy people paying big money for someone to walk their dogs a few times a week. I believe you get the idea. You can use whatever talent you have to get the extra money you need.

Your private lessons can be advertised to family, friends or colleagues and various sites online such as Craigslist, USFreeads.com or do a search in any of the major search engines such as Google for "free sale listings" and you'll get more than enough websites to list your items. The various social media platforms such as Facebook marketplace are also really good places to post. Let's not forget about the church, mosque, synagogue, temple, or other places of worship. You can even make some flyers and post them in your community centers, grocery store bulletin boards, apartment complex front offices and so forth. Be clear on what services you are offering as well as terms and price. Include your telephone number and address where you can be reached.

When you provide the first few services to very satisfied customers, ask their permission to use them as references. It's all about using resources at your disposal to further your agenda. So far, we covered the role a job or a second job plays in the scheme of things. We even made it a point to locate any leaks in spending habits and plug it as the examples in luxury cars and excessive homes demonstrates a missed opportunity. Finally, we explored talents or special skills that one might tap in order to move forward. Now let us look at personal belongings that are of no use to you. Make a quick assessment of your personal belongings and evaluate what you need and what you can do without and even what can be easily downgraded. Remember this strategy is intended to get money into your hands quickly for a bigger cause.

Use Resources at your Disposal

Gather the things you can do without that are operable and in good condition. Examples of such things are electronics, furniture, toys, used books, machinery, lawn equipment, jewelry, unused vehicles, and even a vacant room in your house can be rented with background, credit, and reference checks performed prior to move in. Everyone may have different possessions but the principles remain the same. For items to be resold, be sure to clean and perform maintenance on it before sale if applicable. The idea is to liquidate these items quickly so you will have cash or monthly ongoing cash.

Now that you have items to sell, it's time to put these things in front of buyers. Any of the following are suitable for selling things fast. It is a principle of mine to always find the path of least resistance no matter the circumstances. In other words, do things the smart and easy way. If you agree, start by telling all your friends and associates that you have items for sale as part of a fundraiser for a business. Keep in mind, this is not the right time to give your possessions away for free, as we'll cover charity in the final chapter. You can also organize a yard sale, either stand-alone or with other members of your community as well as use all the other methods of free advertising covered in the paragraph about private lessons. While pawn shops will give you immediate cash on demand, let that be your last option since they usually pay very low. Additional options include a flea market and online auctions such as eBay.

To be certain that you're getting a fair price, visit eBay.com and do a search for similar items. A 10 percent reduction is advisable. There you have it, a few practical strategy to help you profit from your personal belongings. You now know exactly how to turn these items into money. When you have figured out how to profit from selling your own services and products, duplicate it as many times as feasible and you are on your way to success. Furthermore, make it your agenda to form mutual partnerships with others for the sole purpose of profiting from their services and products. Since we're focusing at this point on creating money out of nothing, this method will rely on your ability to successfully execute the previous methods. If so, you'll have no problem doing this as well. The idea is to approach family, friends, neighbors, and other members of your community and make them an offer to sell their unused personal belongings on consignment.

It is advisable to draft a quick single page agreement and include things such as service or product description, condition, price, time frame for sale, and other terms you see necessary. Include a section for signatures for both parties involved, then clean and perform maintenance on all items for sale if applicable and follow the instructions outlined above.

Monetize Education and Training

Your professional education and experiences are also key factors in terms of strategizing your higher grade services. Everyone's case is unique so take a quick assessment: What formal higher education do you have and what work do you do or have done professionally? Can it be quickly monetized and where? These are the primary set of questions you will have to examine to get a clear direction of what is realistic for you in terms of structure. Proceed to do this exercise so you can see the potential professional services that can quickly be monetized.

For those without formal higher education or professional experience, I've still got you covered. No skills are required for grocery delivery, car washing services, house painting, cleaning service, window cleaning, ride sharing like Lyft, Uber, plastic and scrap metal recycling. Any of these mentioned can be easily done for extra cash.

Designs for business cards, flyers, brochures, logos and much more can all be done for you for only five dollars on Fiverr.com. You can market and get orders from offline businesses in your community at a set price and get them completed for five dollars. Go to any printing shop and get them printed for your customers. Be sure to price them correctly so that there's profit after you pay for the design and printing. Take a down payment so you'll have money to use as payment is required before any design can be made on the website mentioned above.

A remote secretary, better known as a virtual assistant or VA is yet another option for extra cash although it may not be suitable for people with full-time jobs. Particular skills that come to mind in terms of being a VA is a strong communication, writing, and interpersonal skill. VA may answer and make phone calls, prepare documents, fax and receive faxes, or do a specific assigned task such as data entry. This type of service is versatile and usually company-specific training is provided if needed. This job can be done from home or away from the company's physical location. It is, therefore, suitable especially for people that want to earn money working from home. Some may even provide video training via Skype.

Other Miscellaneous Ways

Having a smartphone can also earn you money. There are numerous free apps that pay you for completing some minor task such as surveys, sharing photos, secret shopping and watching videos. They are all flexible which means you can do it at your leisure. You can look up apps like Ebates, Book scouter, iPoll and Loot to see if any of it is right for you.

The smartphone can also be used for online video, a concept where you can record some helpful information on regular basis and place them on YouTube. With some proven strategies, your views will increase and you'll begin to make money with ads. The key is to create useful videos that people actually want to watch. Simply create an account and use your Smartphone to record the videos. You can find instructions on account setup and how to create videos on right there on YouTube.

Other ventures that can render you extra cash such as cleaning services and landscaping services should not be overlooked as these can also put immediate cash into your account. With many of these ventures, you can negotiable prices even before the job commences and you are paid when the job is done. If you make a simple flyers or yard signs and post them in heavy traffic areas in your community, you will be contacted for inquiries but you should know in advance the reasonable charges per square foot, and what's included etc. to avoid unforeseen problems from occurring. There are tens and even hundreds of other great initial cash ideas just like the ones I've mentioned that can be tapped. You are only limited by your lack of imagination and creativity.

The examples given in this chapter are intended to activate the creativity within you on your quest to generating initial cash. There are limitless ideas that you'll discover as you begin to explore your talent, skills, and interest. Remember, you are an asset and that means you have the potential to make money. Any idea you choose can be duplicated but keep in mind that growing your asset and limiting your liabilities is a key recipe for success. The amount of money needed to start your structured business is dependent on the type of business you choose. Be reminded, there are some tax responsibilities and it will be covered in a later chapter.

Sound Assets Begins with Correct Structure

I really want you to get comfortable with the term asset and the fact that it will make you money. In other words, a correctly structured asset has an economic value. The good news is that there are no shortages of assets. Some assets will generate more money than others. Besides a moderate home, transportation, utilities, and a few other necessities, all of your earnings and income should be used to acquire assets. It is wise to look at things surrounding you with a business lenses.

Another way to look at asset is everything you owe (liability) and everything you own (equity) makes it up. Naturally, that means that all unnecessary liabilities have to be eliminated. When that happens, more money is made available to buy more assets. I cannot overemphasize this first concept in creating a business Roadmap to success. You'll see this again and again as you read further. Buy what will make you money, not what will consume money.

When you travel from point A to B in unfamiliar locations, a road map or GPS is used to make sure you don't get lost along the way. The same logic should be used in any new business. It should be organized and well defined so that anyone with an elementary education can follow. In your absence, your business should continue to operate if done correctly, it certainly should outlive you, like companies such as AT&T, Walmart, McDonald's, Sony, Gucci, Toyota, Levi, Universal, KLM, and Apple etc. I'm sure with its structure and positioning, others like Google, Microsoft, Facebook and even Starbucks will outlive its original founders too.

These types of entities are well formulated and its trademarks are registered. They take branding extremely serious and stay ahead with innovations and tend to plan ahead for at least 5, 10, 15 and 25 years. A good investor keeps track of what his/her competition is doing and uses technology to stay ahead. They conduct research studies in key areas of their business. A lot of these companies partner with the best financial firms to assist them as well as their employees with various types of investment. Often, the trendsetters are those that not only forecast the future but dictates what the future will be in terms of product and service utilization.

Your choice of business as a beginner should be one that requires little fund for startup but scalable and is accompanied by simplistic operation policy. Even the initial process should be profitable and operable with minimum staff. With the exception of stocks and bonds or other forms of security investments, do not assemble a business that doesn't become profitable within a few months and certainly no more than 6 months. Even a residential real estate acquisition which often requires waiting period and repairs should be executed properly so that you see profits in no more than six months.

Seek to Solve a Problem

Your basis for starting a business is to provide a solution to something and do it better than anyone else. Solve a problem by making people's life easier or better, make things convenient, bigger or stronger, create a shortcut to a complex problem, save lives, use your creativity to develop a technology or help people in other ways. One of the first set of questions one should answer is the need and marketability when starting a business. Do people genuinely have a need for this type of product or service? Can I successfully market it to potential customers?

You must dig deeper by checking the targeted demography to see how they feel about it and most importantly if this is something that will help them. How much potential does this business have in terms of profit is determined by the revenue minus the cost of goods sold. When the cost of goods goes up, your profit goes down. You can always find more efficient ways to produce but it must be profitable in your calculus.

Make a determination of the startup cost. I mean everything needed to successfully open for business must be considered. I am talking about the space, the physical setup and all that it entails, the inspections and licenses, the inventory if applicable, the staff if applicable, the marketing, and the training if needed. How will this business be funded? Will the money be self-funded, come from a lender, an investor, a family or friends? How much is to be used for startup and how much for operating cost must be figured early on to avoid mismanagement.

It is also a pre-checklist item to see if there are others in this industry and if so how they are doing. The last thing you want to do is engage in a business that is over saturated or on a decline. Who are the customers and how will they be reached is a question that must be answered early on. This is how the business will generate revenues so do the research.

People will do business with you if they know and trust you so meeting and surveying people is a great start.

Know what is required to become fully operational because this fact cannot be overlooked. Having the space set up and the product or service may be minuscule as opposed to what remains to be completed before the first sale. You must know what permits are required from your city, county, state, federal and licensing agencies. These things can take time so proper information will help in coordinating so time is not wasted.

Selecting a Physical Location

When starting a physical business, always research starting with deed restriction checks and zoning laws. It eliminates the chances of being blindsided. Deed restrictions are usually in full effect when cities have no zoning laws. Due to the fact that communities have their own deed restrictions, it varies from sub-division to sub-division. I should mention that enforcement however still comes from the city.

It is vital to own your building whenever possible. With a great credit, income, collateral, and a few other requirements, you can secure a separate loan for the business property and for operation. Doing it this way ensures that you build equity for yourself not your landlord. There are cases where you'll have to lease a space. That arrangement should be temporary and moving into your own building at the end of your lease should be incorporated into your plan.

If you do lease, negotiate free rent for at least 6 months or until all permits and licenses to operate have been received. Typically, it takes that long to get build out permits, complete the work, have inspections conducted, receive a certificate of occupancy, set up the business and have all final inspections completed by licensing agencies. Also, ask the landlord to pay for one hundred percent of the build-out cost. This is very important since the build out is permanent and cannot be taken with you at the end of the lease.

Sign all lease documents with your properly protected company name. Never sign a personal guarantor. Call the light and water company for service after lease has been signed, then connect telephone and security alarm after completion of build out. It is also important to get your signs as early as possible. Front signage, roadside sign and door sign with hours of operation and telephone number can all serve as advertising during the construction.

Doing Business As (DBA) or an Assumed Name is a county requirement that must be filed. This filing is good for 10 years in most states. Although you register a name within your county, it is not preserved therefore others can eventually use the same name. Contact your local county for registration information.

License and Permit Requirements

Sales Tax Permit is a state mandate for businesses that sell or provide taxable products or services. This means that you cannot legally operate without it. I should mention that most states will fine you for each day your business operates without a sales tax permit. Contact your state comptroller for details for filing information.

Employer ID Number (EIN) or Federal Tax ID is required if you have one or more employees. If you do not have any employees, you may use your social security number. Filing for an EIN is done through the Internal Revenue Service or IRS. Contact IRS for your Federal Tax ID Number.

Some counties require that a rendition tax be filed on the business personal property. It includes assets such as company vehicles, inventory, furniture, equipment, and machinery. Any property with a real value must be rendered taxable. Contact your County Appraisal District for filing instructions.

Certain permits have to be attained from your city when you acquire a commercial building of some type. Among them are Fire Marshall Permit, Sign Permit, Certificate of Occupancy, Burglar Alarms and others. Each city has its own unique requirements. Contact your city permitting department for a detailed list of permit and licensing agencies.

Depending on the type of business you choose, additional licenses and/or permits may be required. For instance a real estate license for a Realtor and a state bar license for a law firm and so many others. The sure thing to do is to contact your state for a specific license requirement.

Federal regulations may also apply to your particular business. I will not attempt to name all the federal agencies such as Securities & Exchange Commission, Food & Drug Administration, and Federal Trade Commission that may have a direct effect on your business. Simply visit Business.usa.gov for more information.

It must be understood that if you employ at least one person, you have mandated state and federal agencies obligations to fulfill. Among some of these agencies are Equal Employment Opportunity Commission, Social Security Administration, Department of Labor, Citizenship & Immigration Services, Occupation Safety & Health Administration State Unemployment Compensation and others. There are required posters pertaining to laws and statutes that must be clearly visible to employees at the workplace. For specifics, visit DOL.gov for the latest information.

Common Business Structures

Let me say this, I am not a lawyer so please consult legal advice from a licensed attorney when dealing with such matters. The information's here are to show you current popular structures that can be adopted. If your business is not DBA filed with your local county, then it can take one of the following legal structures. Here is a list of each and an explanation to accompany them.

The first and most common structure is sole proprietorship. Being a sole proprietor means you own it all from assets to liabilities of your business. In the event of your death, no one has to assume your liabilities besides what's accumulated in your estate. Single income tax filings are appropriate for this type of structure with no distinction between personal and business debt.

When the above business structure is shared among two or more people, it is called a general partnership. It requires a separate entity and personal assets of all partners. All assets and liabilities are equally shared by all parties. As a result, a separate partnership income tax return has to be filled annually. When a general partnership is registered, it is called a registered limited liability partnership. With this, a partner avoids personal liability caused by other partners.

When you want a separation between your personal assets and business ventures, a corporation is the way to go. In other words, a corporation is its own entity, therefore a sense of personal safety exist in terms of assets. For tax purposes, it can be formed as a C Corporation or S Corporation. The difference being, the first is tax at a higher rate while the latter passes on the burden to the owners themselves.

If I were to be biased, I would choose an LLC or Limited Liability Company due to its simplicity and flexibility especially when two or more people enter a business venture. As the name implies, this type of structure provides limited liability to its owners. Although an LLC is unincorporated, it has some aspect of an S corporation and taxes are filed at the individual owner's level.

Some of the benefits of properly structuring your entity are tax deductions. A write off up to twenty-five thousand dollars for a company vehicle is permissible as well as mileage deductions for work-related activities. As always, make sure you maintain a log as you're allowed fifty-five cents a mile. Your entity will enjoy one hundred percent health premiums and healthcare deductibles such as medical insurance and doctor visits or procedures. Be sure to stipulate that your company offers health insurance by using the keyword "medical reimbursement plan".

With a corporation, you can pay for birthday parties, holiday gifts, vacation, clothes, and tuition tax-free. Additionally, you can get tax free when you hire your kid's of ages 7-17years and pay up to five thousand nine hundred and fifty dollars. They pay no payroll tax and your business gets a deduction as well. While enjoying these tax breaks, your children are learning how to take care of assigned responsibilities at the same time. Their assignment may vary based on your business. Examples of some task the kids could do includes cutting grass, envelope stuffing and labeling, cleaning the office, scanning, shredding and filing documents etc. It is extremely important that you keep a log of all work duties they perform and the frequency or schedule. Here are steps to keep you on track:

1. Create an entity (LLC or S-Corporation)

2. Give your kids a job- some of their potential responsibilities are listed above

3. Open a bank account for the child

4. Pay into the child's bank account if you have an LLC

5. No need for the child to file a tax return

6. No need for you to file w2, 1099, FICA, or worker's compensation

7. For S-Corporation, setup FMC or family management company

8. Pay the fee to the FMC, then FMC can pay it to child's bank account

9. FMC will file a schedule C for expenses and outside labor, if you have an S-Corp

10. Kids 18 years and older do not apply. Pay them and do a 1099 or w2

Employer Responsibilities

Some of the employer's responsibility are listed below. Your tax accountant can bring you up to speed on the current rates and requirements. Although social security and Medicare are paid by employees, you as the employer must match it. In other words, you will match the current rate of 6.2 percent of social security tax and 1.45 percent of the Medicare tax for a total of 12.4 and 2.9 percent. These percentages are important as they are part of your payroll expenses. Having just a few employees keeps payroll cost down. You have no cost in federal tax but are responsible for deducting it and sending it to the IRS via form 941 every quarter. Form 1099 is for anyone you pay that is not a regular employee. An example would be a contractor.

1. Social security

2. Medicare

3. Federal tax

4. State tax (if applicable)

5. Unemployment insurance

6. Form 940

7. Form 941

8. Form 1040 for Sole proprietor

9. Form 1065 for partnership

10. Form 1099

A corporation by name sounds good and big but in essence, it's just having the correct structure of protection. That's what it's all about. When you incorporate your business, it separates it from your personal belongings such as your home, land, automobiles, bank account, and other investments. Other protection you may need includes but not limited to workers compensation insurance, general liability insurance, auto insurance, property insurance and surety bond. Although your attorney will work with you to prepare legal documents, it's good for you to be familiar with the process of the following.

1. Incorporating your business

2. Issuance of shares

3. Selecting the board of Directors

4. Designing organizational chart

5. Recording minutes

6. Writing bylaws

7. Writing company policy

8. Writing a standard operating procedure

9. Writing emergency evacuation and lock down plan

10. Writing best practices

The more familiar you are, the more input you can have with item 1 to 6, however, item 7 to 10 will mostly be your policies although your attorney will make sure it's legal. Be sure to include opening, closing, normal day procedures, pay period, attendance, wage, and salary etc. in your policies. Include job duties and responsibilities as well as hours of operation.

Negotiating the Lease

Take great care when negotiating the lease or purchase of your space. A huge amount of money can be saved if done tactfully. If you're not comfortable with negotiations, it would be better to use a Realtor to communicate your wish. Also insist on at least 6 months free lease or until all permits and licenses to operate have been received. Often at times during the build-out, an unforeseeable delay may occur that can last several months. It does not make any sense to start paying rent during construction. Imagine paying ten thousand dollars for several months before your store opens for business. You would not be a happy camper. It is therefore imperative to allow yourself contingency in terms of time and money during your planning phases.

Ask the landlord to pay 100 percent of the build-out cost. Again, this step is doable if you are determined to run your business in the most efficient manner. Build-out or tenant improvement cost can easily range from one hundred thousand to several hundred thousand on a commercial shell building. Agreeing to pay even twenty-five percent of it can cost you tens of thousands. You may have an expensive setup depending on the type of business so save your money for it. Anyway, all the several costs in terms of equipment & machinery, construction and operating capital would have to be defined in your elaborate business plan.

Be certain you sign all lease documents with your properly protected company name and never sign with your name or sign a personal guarantor. Listen, if you fail to protect yourself, no one will. Take measures to ensure that you separate yourself from your newly formed corporation. If the landlord insists that you sign your name or personal guarantor on the lease documents, explain to them that you are only representing the company as a manager or a director. As part of the asset protection that we've discussed, the corporation must conduct its own business legally. The corporation is run by people, who act as representatives of it. It should be a deal breaker if they make it mandatory for you to sign your name. Do not do it. I hope I'm clear on this crucial step.

Tenant Improvement

During the lease negotiation, It is good to go ahead and request 3 bids from general contractors. These contractors should be experienced with doing this type of tenant improvement build-out that's needed. The first thing you must do is verify and validate their business license. Next, you should ask for three referrals from each bidder. Go ahead and check these referrals. As I mentioned before, this type of project takes a lot of money and time so you do not want to be stuck with someone that is unprofessional, non-communicative or simply incompetent. Doing your due diligence correctly will uncover any potential issues that could arise.

If both the license and referrals check out, you may begin the negotiation. Negotiate for a turnkey solution. That means the contractor you chose must handle everything from architectural drawings and work permits to inspections and certificate of occupancy. You will be too busy to babysit any contractor. The contractor must agree to your terms in writing. If you want something and it is not in writing, you most likely won't get it. Although the contractor has agreement forms that will detail every aspect of the job, you are free to make changes to the forms and have them initial and sign those changes.

Stipulate the payment intervals and be sure not to release more than fifty percent of the entire amount until you have a certificate of occupancy in your hands. It is assumed that a professional contractor has the capital to begin the job before demanding the first payment. Break it into three or four phases and release funds after the completion of each phase. Certificate of occupancy is the only thing that gives you permission to open your place of business, and you can't get it until all inspections are passed.

Put contingency clause in place to make sure contractors stick to the timeline. Put another one that penalizes the contractor if the job is not finished at least 1 week after the proposed completion date. You can charge the contractor fifty percent of what you expect to make when you open. For instance, you could include in the agreement that the contractor will pay you a thousand dollars per day if he fails to complete the job one week after the due date. When you run your business like a business, they will know you mean business and do all they can to meet the stipulated deadlines. They will not neglect your build-out for other jobs.

Do perform a walk-through with the contractor after the job is completed. Remember the inspectors are there to inspect code and safety aspects of the tenant improvement. Your job is to check to see if all the specifications, add-on and cosmetics are completed per agreement. Do not release the final payment until everything is completely done per the agreement. Check the walls, ceiling tiles, floor, plumbing, electrical, fire alarm system, paint, and any other item that was to be completed. Additional setup include installation of light, water, phone, security alarm, furniture, office equipment, and appliances. Front Signage, door sign and roadside sign with hours and telephone number should already be in place as it serves as advertising while the build-out is taking place. These can be the responsibility of the contractor as long as is agreed upon per the contract. Write the final check when everything is correct and proceed with other functions.

Hire the Best

When it comes to employees, hire the best talents and perform a background check, credit check, and routine drug check if applicable.

Look for talents that are suitable for the type of business you are establishing. Hire the best and make sure you do not discriminate on the basis of race, gender, nationality, disability, and others outlined by Equal Employment Opportunity Commission or its equivalent in your country. Be sure to also follow labor laws by hiring people that are age appropriate and legally permissible to work in your country. Be sure to pay above minimum wage as you will get more out of your team if you give them the incentive to do more.

Ask each candidate for three professional references and three personal. Expect the personal ones to sing their praises. The professional references, on the other hand, tend to be more upfront about their experience with your candidates. Follow the law on what you can and cannot ask as you conduct your reference checks. Simply introduce yourself and ask if the manager can talk for a few minutes. Proceed to tell them the reason for the call. Use your own style but be sure to start by asking if they know your candidate. Ask them their relationship with your candidate and what job duties they performed while employed there. Finish your inquiry by asking if the candidate is qualified for rehire. When an employer says no to that question, it is a clear signal that should not be taken lightly.

Those that get passed this stage can now be scheduled for a formal interview. There is no need to waste time performing interviews until you can learn a few things about your potential employee. Screening your applicants like this will save both parties an enormous amount of time and cease any false hopes. During the interview, ask questions that's designed to give insight into who there are and look for consistency and good work ethics. Attendance is always a big issue so dig deep to ensure that your applicants don't have a serious problem with attendance. Make sure the people you select are able to work as scheduled and execute their duties with little or no supervision.

Select your employees and leave a few on a reserve list and set time for training and orientation. During this period, cover the company's policies for operation, safety, emergency, attendance, lock-down, customer service and others. Be sure to have the employees complete all necessary forms such as tax forms, employment eligibility forms, and other industry-specific forms. In fact it is good to keep a master checklist to make sure all items are covered. You must have salary or wage agreement that includes job title and description, frequency and method of payment. Have a dress code so your brand remains consistent. Ensure that your entire staff knows the chain of command.

Test Your Marketing Efforts

Smart and Strategic marketing allows the management to track the sources of their sales. Surveys and questionnaires also play a big part. With online marketing, you can easily with digital imprints such as clicks and impressions depending on the type of biz, having a result driven marketer on staff is invaluable. Marketing material must clearly identify a problem and then offer a solution. Marketing materials should always spark emotions and sell a destination. In other words, what your product or service will do for your potential customers.

According to television producer and marketing consultant Blair Warren, "people will do anything for those who encourage their dreams, justify their failures, allay their fears, confirm their suspicion, and help them throw rocks at their enemies. "Advertising companies have sales copywriters that understand this psychology and should be considered for consultation. When you have talents that can produce results, it is better to use them than to do it yourself, if you have no experience it that department.

Remember sales equals' money so paying for more sales is a smart business and highly advisable. If you give great incentives to your customers, they will refer your business to others and soon you would have created a formidable referral machine. You can do similar incentives for your staff to also refer customers. Multiple marketing campaigns should be tested with those that bring results continuously. When it comes to marketing, nothing should be ruled out unless it's not working or feasible.

A certain amount of education and work is required in your quest to be financially successful. For education, there is no substitute as you should be knowledgeable in all of your business ventures. Perhaps spending some time and money on educating yourself is truly priceless. Although you are going to employ the best, it is just as important to be very familiar with the operation of your business. Rather than building their own brand from the ground up, many elect to buy a franchise. With a little research, you can uncover the overall performance of a franchise, its commitment to franchisees and its fees. It's a viable option for many because in most cases it has a profitable track record with processes already in place.

When it comes to securing a business loan, your local credit union provides better packages than the big name financial institutions. Always check their rate and terms first before going anywhere else. It is very important to apply for a fixed rate loan anytime you borrow long term with multiple years of payback. A smart investor only chooses variable rate if it's for a short term. Apart from the credit union, check with your local Small Business Administration or SBA for lenders that follow their guidelines.

Every single business can benefit from strategic promotions. Whether its sweepstakes, contest, free trial, samples, or buy one get a second at a discounted rate, incorporating a promotion will increase revenues. Be observant next time you visit your local grocery store and you'll see all the types of promotions taking place from coupons to free samples. They do it because it works. Make promotions part of your business strategy and use the most effective ones that yield the best ROI.

A good customer experience will boost sales with virtually every business. Your policy must emphasize service first and sales second. Train employees to adhere to your policy at all times. We all value our time therefore quick service is also very necessary. Being helpful, quick and running a physically clean operation are all compulsory if you are to be superior in customer service. Increase sales and referrals are all direct evidence of good customer service.

Make a decision on where and when the business will be operated, by how many people and strategic location. When you make things convenient for your customers, they will do business with you. Taking payments are included in making things easy for your customers so give them multiple ways to pay. At a minimum, you should accept cash, check, money order, and credit cards. If you have a recurring service that is paid on a weekly or monthly basis, consider bank draft or EFT as well.

The break-even point is also essential. Every serious business should be able to perform a break-even analysis. This is simply money spent and money made in layman terms. In other words, if it cost you nothing to provide a service, you'll reach a break-even point and make a profit as soon as you're paid. When you have a cost, however, you will calculate it using fixed cost divided by the average price per unit minus average cost per unit. Using this formula will enable accurate projections of when your business can support itself.

How easy will it be to expand when the need arises or liquidate if it does not work out? Starting small does not mean staying that way for months or years to come. Knowing that, businesses must have a system in place to facilitate expansion. It is for the prevention of future headaches associated with the growth of a company. All the same, you also plan for the possibility of going out of business. An exit plan is compulsory and should be defined. If the need arises, will you sell the business itself or sell the components of the business or simply shut down? The question of how to do it must be clear.

Business Exploratory Research

Before starting a business of any kind, you must conduct an exploratory research. At a minimum, the research must include methods such as interviews, case studies, and team discussions. It is a good idea to review financial records of a similar business if accessible. Public companies have shareholders and therefore must disclose their statement of earnings and other agreed files to the public. Private firms, however, are not required by the Security and Exchange Commission to do so. For investments of any kind, so long as the company is publicly traded, you can visit the investor relations tab of the company's website and examine its financial records. Knowing how to read a financial statement is key however your CPA can give you a professional analysis of these documents. Financial reports should paint a picture of growth and profitability for the period of time. I would look as far back as ten years if available.

Case studies should be conducted to see what products or services are offered, successes and failures, overall cost, pricing, and ultimately ROI. Team discussions will enable a variety of perspectives on the subject. The scope of interviews should include potential customer validation of the product or service. For tangible products, create a prototype so that the customers can touch and feel it. Many other indicators can be uncovered during the prototype testing phase. Document your potential customer's reaction to the product and its price point. Answer a very important question, will they buy? If the consensus suggests customers will buy, you've got a good start.

For the smaller privately own companies, setting an appointment to visit and talk to the owner or manager will shed light on internal operations of the business. The management will most likely talk to you as long as you're not planning to be their competition. Select a similar business far from your intended area and make it clear when you communicate with the manager. Explaining what you want to do and that should alleviate any fear of you taking their customers.

Typically you want to establish your brick and mortar in a well-populated area. Whether residential, commercial or a mixture depends on the type of business you wish to start. Be that as it may, conduct the automobile traffic and foot traffic observation on your street. This collection of information will serve as yet another tool for gauging the appropriateness of the location. Refrain from acquiring a place in or near war zones. Most city websites have information's on problematic areas and the activity level of crime.

Visibility is equally as important. It is better to pay a little more in a very visible area with a street view. If your customers cannot find you, they cannot buy. Even within a building, certain parts are more visible than others. Put yourself in front of the customer by going for the best possible spot. All of the above-mentioned factors and much more has to be taken into account before you make the decision on location.

Your CPA, without disclosing anyone confidential financial records can tell you the businesses that tend to do well. They can give you lots of insights and help you get closer to a decision. It is up to you to ask the type of questions that will quench your thirst. For instance what type of performance do you want to see? Just because a business can make a profit does not mean it's going to be worth your time and effort. You can easily earn ten to fifteen percent on the stock market without doing much work besides research and networking. Knowing this makes more sense to strive for upward of twenty percent or higher in profits for small businesses. If you can get all your investment out by the second year, you are on the right track. This is what we call infinite returns after the second year.

Section II
A MILLION DOLLAR LINE

CHAPTER FOUR

Build Business Systems of Success

*Research is key when it comes to
building a sustainable business*

In chapter 2, I showed you a number of ways to pay off your house in as little as five years. If you do it, you'll have one hundred percent ownership of your home's equity. The average home in America cost about two hundred thousand dollars. You would have that amount or more to use as leverage. In addition, you would have generated some initial capital and established great credit. Follow up by completing market research and construct a business roadmap. Leveraging these efforts and capital to attract potential investors or to secure a business loan should now be very easy. The subject of leverage in its simplest term is using less of your own resources and more of others resources to solve a problem for the masses. When this solution is tied into a business model, the end results are mass profits. It all starts however with properly educating yourself. There's nothing worse than not being able to answer essential questions regarding the business you intend to start. Investors and lenders will feel confident when they see a competent plan that illustrates potential profitability. Remember your goal is to have one million dollars or more in lines of credit.

Everything you have done to this point should be captured clearly and systematically in your overall business plan. It should begin with an executive summary that tells the reader exactly what you want to accomplish. Give a description and be sure to include where you see your business in the next few years. You are basically summarizing everything that's included in your business plan. This is regarded as the most important part of plan. It is intended to capture your lender or investors interest which will in turn make them want to know more by reading all of your document.

In a previous chapter, I also stated the importance of market research. All the results of your industry analysis should follow your executive summary including your company, your competition, and your customers. Doing your due diligence on your market will place you in a strategic position where you can grab your share of sales. How you are going to develop your product or service along with advantages and disadvantages should be stated here. Strengths and weaknesses of your competition will enable you to strategize for complete gain. It is a good idea to also show trends in the industry and how you plan to stay abreast of it to retain customers.

Next, state how you are going to develop and market the products or services. Take a branding position and explain your development strategy complete with a feasible budget. You must propose a pricing point that is competitive and enables profitability. This section is not complete until you clearly show how you are going to reach your customers. Your tactics must be sound and practical.

A section that identifies management and operation is essential as it highlights the logistics of the business. Everyone's role within your management should be identified and accompanied by an organizational chart. Each person should be charged with his or her responsibility within the organization. Be sure to show how the business will function on a day to day basis. Where you intend to be in the next few years as far as operation with capital and expense outlined.

Your final section is your financial plan. State how much funding is needed and how it will be utilize. If you remember in chapter 2, I wrote that lenders will want to be sure that they will get their money back. It is now time to show them growth with numbers. How much will you spend on assets and what revenues you expect in the next one to five years should all be shown at this point. This financial forecast will also aide you in running your business more effectively.

The single biggest mistake is to limit one's self and not invest in other viable and profitable businesses. Brick and mortar, like online or any other business, should be equipped with a team that includes but not limited to a realtor, a lawyer, and accountant, a personal assistant, a mentor, and staff, if applicable. Take your time when assembling this team as many will be with you for a lifetime. Make sure each member is vetted and there exist no conflict of interest. Moreover, pay attention to the personalities of each prospect. Collectively, your team will make your ventures a success so build a mutually respected relationship with them. Although the duty of most of the players on your team is self-explanatory, I will explain to ensure we are all on the same page, no pun intended!

The purpose of your lawyer is to give ongoing counsel and legal advice so you can stay abreast of the current rules, regulations, policies, changes, and best practices etc. They will draw, negotiate, and interpret contracts on your behalf. When you have an attorney on your team, you will avoid many unforeseen problems from occurring while having the confidence that any future legal issue will be handled by a competent person whom you trust.

An accountant on your team means complicated tax code and number crunching is a non-issue. They can get things done much quicker, professionally, and with less scrutiny from the IRS. Your accountant should perform services such as calculating your assets, equity, and liability. They should file all necessary local, state, and federal income tax. Even with an accountant, it is still important that you stay organize and maintain a book for all business related transactions.

A Realtor for any brick and mortar business enables owners to operate more efficiently in terms of searching for a physical location. Besides finding you a place, your realtor will review all closing documents given by the landlord or lender before you sign them. In essence, they are your protection as far as not signing a bad mortgage or lease. Still yet, realtors have a tool that does a multitude of research and analysis about your business area. Among these tasks are traffic count, demographics, average cost per square feet in the area, future developments and much more. For the percentage they charge, which is usually paid by the seller, it is simply not smart to search for a place nor sign a mortgage or lease without a realtor.

Time is money and having your own secretary or personal assistance saves you an ample amount of time. Throughout this book, you've read that it is better to focus on those tasks that brings revenue into your business. In other words, what generates little or no income should be handled by your personal assistant. Examples of such duties are clerical, lead generation, errands, and low level meetings. Do not confuse personal assistant with staff.

The need for staff is determined by looking at a few factors. If your business requires cashiers, customer service representatives, salesman, or other qualified professionals like technicians and the like, then you need staff. You can manage your staff initially but the idea is to eventually promote them from within if possible or hire a manager. Do not waste valuable times trying to do it all because you'll lose money and may even become exhausted. Be realistic in deciding what human resources are needed and the role of each.

Last but not least, every business owner must have a mentor. This person can be anyone that has successfully done what you're trying to do. Do not settle when choosing a mentor or in that case any member of your team. Instead, select someone with extensive knowledge that you can trust. The days of trial and error are long gone. It is not smart to figure things out on your own in business, beside you'll waste too much time and may end up closing your business without the proper guidance. Choose a mentor from the same industry and do not compete directly with them. This way, they'll be more receptive to helping you out.

Business Plan

Every serious business must have a business plan. Even if you've managed to be somewhat successful, you'll need a business plan when you decide to expand. It highlights key aspects of your business and is required by financial institutions. At a minimum, a business plan should include 5 years of projected growth. Here is an example of page one and the table of content followed by a breakdown of the various sections that constitutes a business plan. All sections does not have to be exact however all aspect of the business must be captured in your plan.

I. Cover Letter

This is the first section of the plan. An established business will have a much more detailed plan however this is for a new business. Include the dollar amount that you intend to borrow, duration and terms of the loan, type of funding you want.

II. Executive Summary

The summary gives the reader a quick picture of your entire plan. It should include business name, location and description, products/services, market, competition and management qualifications.

Business goals should be clearly stated. Be sure to list any financial needs and how funds will be allocated to each need. Finally, state expected earnings and how it will be disbursed to investor.

III. Market Analysis

Everyone must do a market analysis of some sort before launching a business. Included in your analysis should be industry and market description with size, trends, geographic considerations, competition and pricing.

IV. Products/Services

Give the reader details of your products and/or services. Be sure to include a description of products or services and how it will benefit consumers. It is important to address patents and other legal or technical factors. Compare and contrast your products/services in respect to that of your competitor. Include manufacturing procedure if applicable.

V. Marketing and Sales Strategy

Define how you intend to market your business. List the overall marketing strategy in terms of sales. Showcase your pricing policy in this section and list the terms of sales. Be sure to list your plans for distributing, selling and servicing.

VI. Organizational and Management Plan

Specify the unique style of your business in terms of organizational and management plan. In other words, show the form of business organization you have including directors or officers if applicable. Include organizational chart with each member's defined responsibility. Having each key personnel resume as part of this plan is also a good idea.

List plans for staffing and payroll with detailing number of employees as well as cost. Any facility and operating plans for the next 5 years should be listed. Be sure to address any government mandate that directly affects your business.

VII.   Financial Data and Projection

It is critical that all borrowers have a financial projection. No financial institution will lend your business money without it. A five year financial history and projections including profit and loss statement, balance sheet, cash flow and estimates for capital expenditure must be listed. Be sure to explain your projections and use of funds and include factors such as key business ratios. Conclude with graphs and charts to illustrate positive trends and list expected returns for investors.

Imagine owning several businesses that generates a million dollars each and every year. Now that you've visualized the idea, it's time to make it a reality. It is really not difficult to be successful in business, just intelligence and persistent. There aren't any limits on ventures that yields attractive returns when you position yourself appropriately. For the same reason, you may see a successful business somewhere but an unsuccessful one of the same type elsewhere. What and how it is operated can make or break it. I'll list a few diverse and known profitable businesses models to give you some ideas. Although these businesses tend to do well, I'm going to show you one or two additional unique selling proposition (USP) to make you stand out and attract relatively more customers.

Business Center Model

This business consists of having a brick and mortar storefront where customers can print, make copies, fax, and access the internet etc. for a fee. Other services that should be incorporated into the print shop are ink/toner refills and being USPS, FedEx, and UPS authorized shipper.

Add a small section for mailboxes. Many home and businesses will rent the mailboxes because they don't want to make their home addresses public. Be sure to sell all related stationery as well since some of the people that visit the store may need such items. Just look at the demographics of consumers that will frequent your store if you cater to their needs. For instance, clients may want phone cards and cell phone accessories as well as gift packaging materials.

Apart from selling a long list of related items, you'll generate income from the core services of printing therefore this business should not be overlooked. Location is a very important factor to consider. Construct your business in a highly populated area that has no such services to enjoy a great return on your investments. Your unique selling proposition (USP) could be having express designers on demand. These designers can handle anything like websites, logo, video production, graphics, marketing materials, writing, programming, voice over and sound effect etc. Your business can contract these services from several reputable online services and charge a markup. You are basically outsourcing these USP's for a profit.

Merchant Services Model

When you operate a merchant services business, you can incorporate other services such as security and alarms. Here is the breakdown of the said model. Virtually every business has to accept payment through a variety of methods other than cash. Merchant services provide credit/debit card terminals and accessories. An attractive means of profit will also derive from the sales of security cameras and monitors. Secure a contract with ADT, the largest company of its type in America and you'll get several thousand dollars per customer sign-up.

As you can see, a firm like this is extremely lucrative with multiple streams of pulling revenues. Move in quickly on new businesses before your competitors do, for they are your primary target. That said, be sure to obtain a listing of all new business fillings from your state. Hire a telemarketer from oversees to offer your services to these businesses. You can find many telemarketers online that speaks English, Spanish, and several other languages. They are usually managed by a company that provides the facility and charge them a fee. Since this is a business to business services (B2B), your USP could be the service of telemarketing which you can attain from your oversee source. Offer all your business customers a telemarketing service for a fee.

Cleaners Model

What comes to mind when you hear the words laundry mart? Perhaps you may think of a place where people go to wash their clothes and other washable belongings for a fee. You are absolutely correct and you can expand your investment into this area for higher profits. This business requires very minimum staffing when compared to others. Establishing a laundry mart is all about location. Set it up in a heavily populated lower income residential area and you'll get all the business you can handle. Your rent or mortgage should be relatively lower as opposed to a middle class neighborhood.

Please keep in mind that modifications to the plumbing and electrical systems will have to be made if you lease a building. Washers and dryers should be purchased with an extended warranty that covers repair or replacement option plan. This way, you can avoid costly repairs after the initial manufacturer's warranty. Pick up the money generated each day and deposit it into your account and within a short time you'll see the value in this business.

As you cruise through the middle class sections of your town, you see people paying for convenience. It is true that people pay for services that they cannot do or just don't have time to do. For majority of the professional workforce, washing their own clothes and ironing them is a bit of an inconvenience. They prefer to drop off their dirty garments and uniforms at the dry cleaners early in the morning before work, then pick it up later in the afternoon after work. People that take their apparels to the cleaners do it in bulk and do so on a consistent basis.

Dry cleaning is very much another viable and profit pulling business that can be tapped into. You can even own and operate this service without having the washing machines at your physical location. It is a practical alternative that many owners are now doing however you'll generate more income with your own equipment. Simply sub-contract with a cleaner and drop off your load in the morning at 10am, then pick it up by 4pm the same day. If calculated correctly, customer who brings their items by 9am can get them back after 5pm on the same day. Most customers will not know nor care that their items are being remotely cleaned. Your USP could be marketing to large firms to pick up their laundry at work in the mornings and delivering them in the evening. It is a convenience that many people would enjoy as its one less stop for customers and it saves them time.

Education/ Care Model

Do you know that with just 50 customers all paying you six hundred dollars a month equals thirty thousand dollars a month? Of course you do, and if the total cost of running the business a month was twenty thousand dollars, you'll earn ten thousand dollars a month in profit. Calculate and you'll get one hundred twenty dollars a year. I must admit, I'm being modest with these numbers because it can quickly double, triple or even quadruple with proper planning.

The subject at hand is preschool/childcare services. It includes full time care, before/after school care, preschool curriculum, tutoring, homework assistance, and physical activities such as karate and dance lessons. Hire qualified care attendants and a program director. Establish a contract with a tutoring, karate and dance studio to have an instructor come in 3 times a week to teach. Coordinate so the instructors are able to use the same room but at different times with just a few quick modifications. Charge parents additional fees for the extra services. Many will be happy to participate because it will help their children's development.

This model can be adopted by anyone who has the ability to employ the educators needed to provide the services. Requirement varies from state to state with a common denominator being background check since they'll be working with children. Qualifications that should be stipulated are prior experience and CPR certification for care attendants and director current certification status for the program director. Thorough research is the key to success in this model. Secure a good location and a very good preschool curriculum.

Check your state requirements and guidelines for classroom to student ratio, care attendant to student ratio, age group configurations and other essentials. It should be located in a heavily populated residential neighborhood with all competitors close by having a waiting list for several age groups. Apart from all these factors, you'll still have the edge by positioning this model strategically. Your USP should be your facility's buses doing pickup and drop offs at the children's residence within a 5 miles radius of the center. Not many are doing this and the ones that do are limited to school age children. You can include all ages.

Deli/Coffee Model

We are living in the age and time where more people demand healthier foods on the go. People also enjoy having a place to hold informal business and student group meeting so a Deli/Coffee shop model is a perfect fit and location is once again a maker or a breaker. My advice is to pick an area with close proximity to downtown, a mall, a major university, or a busy business strip.

The food has to be good, therefore be sure to serve proven selections of Deli and Coffee including an assorted variety of cold drinks. It will surely be a hit since many in the working class like to pick up coffee/tea and pastries on their way to work in the morning.

Some will even buy a deli to take to work for lunch. Pricing should be competitive and quality must be at its highest. Since selling coffee alone is profitable and deli is likewise, you are sure to win by combining the two. Go a step further by adding complimentary internet connection hotspot and watch your shop get flooded with customers daily. With everyone increasingly becoming conscious of their health and well-being, healthy foods, snacks and drinks now receives heavy patronage. Many would rather grab a whole fruit, a vegetable juice or smoothies than a soft drink.

This population is forever increasing so getting into a healthy food business is a no-brainer. Your USP could be an app that can be used to order when customers just leave their house and have their items ready when they arrive. Customers love fast service and don't appreciate waiting so this will attract them. The app can even include additional functions that breaks down the nutritional and health benefits of each item on the menu.

Convenience Store/Gas Station Model

Almost every corner has it yet more corners are being developed with this model in mind. There is a simple reason, it's profitable. The combination of convenience and gas has been around for a long time, raking in huge amounts of cash. Customers that fill up their vehicles will most likely buy other items while at the store. Make it a one stop business by adding an automatic car wash as well as oil change and tire services. The key to this model is location.

As with any of my models, here comes a twist that will put you one step ahead of the competition. Your USP is free 16 ounces coffee or fountain drink to each buying customer. The cost of the free drink is nothing but the rewards are increased foot traffic that comes and purchase from your store. Offering the free drink will gently force customers to come inside. Once they're there, many would buy snacks and other items. Startup cost is on the high side but you'll surely profit in a major way with this model. Pay attention to all the convenient things that customers want and offer them.

Residential Real Estate

Get yourself into the real estate business. Having the notion that this is a bad time for real estate is not accurate. The key to success is planning. Knowing when, where, and how to buy Real estate. For starters search for government bank foreclosures. Like any other business, the purpose of acquiring properties is to make profit. To do it, you must look to buy at nearly fifty percent below market value. This is especially so if you intend repairing and selling or fix and flip as it is commonly referred. If making a substantial profit one property at a time is not your goal, renting is another option that can produce monthly cash flow.

A second strategy that is equally as viable is actively looking for distressed home owners. These owners are delinquent on their mortgage payment or taxes and want a way out. Your purpose is to help them get out without ruining their credit. Most of them may downgrade into an apartment or move in with a family member. Make an offer to pay their delinquent balance or taxes, give them some agreed upon money and take over the mortgage payment. Make sure the owner has adequate equity or else don't do the deal.

If you are a first time home buyer, your focus should be a duplex, triplex or a fourplex. You may be required to live there for at least a year so live in one and rent the rest. The multi-family unit gives you the leverage of paying your mortgage with your tenant's money and having excess cash flow. If you don't like the idea of living with your tenant, move out and rent your apartment after one year.

You may find residential rental property to be quite beneficial but time consuming as you acquire more and more. In that case, you can turn to turnkey solutions. There are companies that does the entire process from finding a property to closing the deal. They even do any repairs needed, rent the property and manage it as well. These turkey home providers usually charge a ten percent management fee.

Doing a combination of renting and flipping will afford you the necessary down payment needed to buy more properties. For instance, after making a twenty thousand dollars profit on a fix and flip, that money can be invested in a rental property. In other words create money and buy assets that continue to pump cash flow into your pocket. There is so much more you can do with residential real estate model such as renting rooms near a college or universities. Your USP could be renting daily or weekly as vacation homes near resorts. Join Airbnb, a company that is disrupting the hotel chains. You can also rent home to companies that does home assisted living for seniors.

Franchise Model

Take a moment to think about establish franchises such Chick-fil-A, Hampton Hotels, H & R Block, 7-Eleven Inc., and Meineke. Do you know what all of these franchises have in common? They all have a tested and proven method of profitability among other important traits. None of them would have been a franchise had they not enjoyed profitable return on investment or ROI. They've indeed done all the ground work by identifying and maintaining a system that works. Anyone who wants to be a part of these franchises have to pay a healthy initial fee plus a percentage of all royalties.

It is also not far-fetched to think about being a franchiser. Plan it from the very beginning of any venture you start so that when your businesses becomes successful, they can be converted into franchises. This is a rich forever way of thinking that has to be understood. You can successfully start a franchise in any industry if you own several lucrative outlets using identical policies and procedures. There are a dozen states or so that requirements have to be met. Your systems has to cover everything such as legal, accounting, daily operation and many other policies and procedures. It is all these processes that made you successful that will be used to transform your business into a franchise. When someone purchase your franchise, they will pay you fees and royalties in exchange for your proven and profitable processes.

Once you've used the skills acquired to establish a business and you're now operating. You have to learn to focus on what absolutely needs your attention and delegate other duties. That means recruit and retain the most talented people. Do not adopt the I can do it all mentality. Spend your time on task that will increase your return on investment and let your team focus on their assigned duties and responsibilities. Franchises are usually very strict in terms of their USP therefore you have to follow it and are not permitted to create your own.

CHAPTER FIVE

Create Processes for Multiple Streams

All serious businesses must automate it's processes and systems wherever possible

Multiple Streams of Income

The power of generating income from multiple sources is one that should never be overlooked. In show business, you can see people like Ryan Seacrest, Steve Harvey, Oprah Winfrey and others wearing a multitude of hats as well as investments and therefore making money in various ways. You can see athletes, entertainers, musicians and other famous people utilizing their platform and celebrity to venture into business for additional revenues. Even highly paid specialized people by profession also follow these strategies and it's not uncommon for a doctor or a lawyer to own their practice when working or own another business not related to their line of work. All these example shows that these people understand the principle of cash flow from several sources.

Devise Wealth System Builder Flowchart

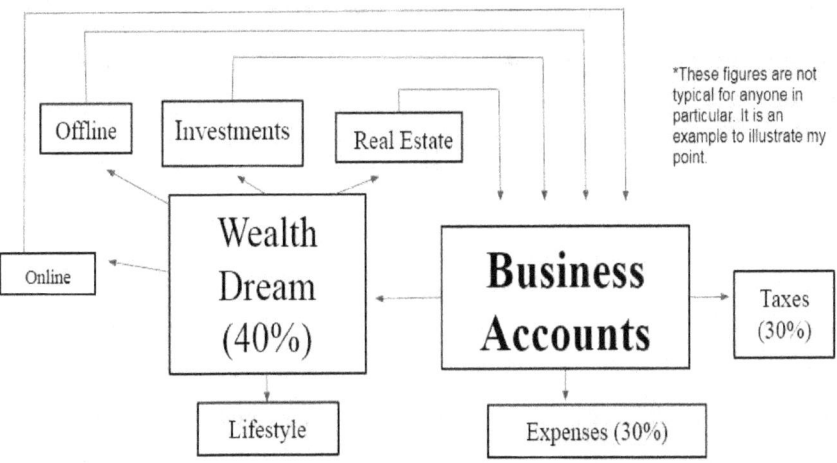

It is clear that all the others that do not fit the description mentioned must also find ways to direct income from a number of sources into their wealth system. At a minimum, besides being an employee, if you're still doing that, there must be passive income from real estate investments, brick and mortar business, online business, and dividends from paper assets such as stocks and bonds. The key is to research each area and have a clear understanding before venturing into it.

No matter who you are and how much you are worth, any acquisition of assets would benefit from the systems and processes Little Money Big Credit. The millionaire celebrity, from athletes to showbiz, performers to musicians, the executives of fortune companies can all use wealth systems and processes to increase and protect wealth. Basically, anyone that reaches the million dollar line and fails to grow and protect it have missed a great opportunity. Even then, starting all over is possible with a new perspective about wealth.

Often, we hear stories of individuals that had it all then suddenly, they lost it all. The misfortune can often be attributed to lack of financial literacy. If a boy who derived from a poverty stricken country with no money, substandard shelter, used clothes and inadequate meals, can rise from such circumstances and have the audacity to educate others, virtually anyone can do the same. It just takes learning and the implementation of necessary actions required to reach your goals.

Profitable Business Acquisition

Anyone that has significant wealth right now but no systems and processes in place can begin by simply researching effective systems and consulting. You have a million dollar credit line and are now looking to capitalize on it. You want to acquire profitable assets that have sound processes and systems already in place. The first step after due diligence is a letter of intent. This document will enable you to have deeper access into the company's internal operation. Go after profitable businesses with the help of your own wealth team. The team should include a business broker, competent business & tax accountant or CPA, a business loan officer, a business lawyer, a business consultant, and an experience business manager. It may seem like a lot of people but you need these experienced professionals help with different aspects of the acquisition. The manager will take care of the hiring, firing, training of staff, operational policies, customer care, payroll, deposit etc. and report directly to you on a weekly, bi-weekly or monthly basis.

Having ran businesses on a smaller scale, your venture into larger acquisition should be a natural progression. You have some experience and have learned many things along the way. Your assets have grown as your credit limit and credit worthiness. You've literally positioned yourself for bigger and better assets that lies ahead. You have built a team of trusted and competent professionals. Your reach is far greater than when you first embarked on the journey to build wealth. People are starting to contact you with business offers.

The luxury of taking the time needed to properly evaluate a businesses is on your side. It should be utilize thoroughly to ensure that arbitration is being used to make your decisions. You are no longer interested in good deals, you want great deals. Just one great opportunity can make you very rich although the idea is to seek to acquire more, but one at time. Apart from all the numbers, buy a business that you understand.

Commercial Real Estate Acquisition

After successfully establishing a profitable business or businesses, the next asset to consider is commercial real estate. There are many forms of commercial real estate with each having its own pros and cons. Among some of the more profitable ones are multi-family units such as apartment complexes. There are others such as office buildings, shopping malls, hotels, strip centers and storage units. All of these properties are profitable and can accelerate your wealth dramatically.

For starters with no experience, as always, your first assignment is to educate yourself on the subject. There are real estate investment groups that does crowd funding. Perhaps you can start there as you learn the ropes and become more familiar. This option is preferred initially because the entry point is significantly low. With as little as five thousand dollars, you can own a part of the investment and receive all the data that pertain to it. Doing it this way will give you a chance to use what you've learned against real time data from your investment.

After collecting cash distribution from income and appreciation, and gaining more experience you can invest more or begin looking into acquiring your own property. Even then, you should partner with an experienced investor before buying one entirely on your own. All these precautions and learning on the job or LOJ should be taken to avoid expensive mistakes. It is better to do multiple ventures with experienced investors than do one on your own if you're inexperienced. After one or two ventures, or when you've gained sufficient experience in commercial real estate deals, go for it and do a sole acquisition.

You need a good team when you decide to buy your own property. Among them are an experienced mentor or consultant, commercial real estate agents and brokers, Lenders, Lawyer, Accountant, Appraiser, Property Management Company, and a good assistant. All members of your team should be experienced. They should also be recommended by your mentor or consultant. This type of acquisition requires a lot of due diligence by a reputable and experienced team. You will have to examine tens of properties, physical as well as the numbers before buying one.

When you study commercial real estate investing, you'll quickly become familiar with factors such as sub-market cap rate, price per unit (door), Expenses per unit (door), and rent for one, two and three bedrooms. You'll be able to take a look at comparable sales data and break it down. Other factors like net operating income or NOI, cash on cash return or ROI, debt coverage ratio or DCR will be properly understood. Looking at properties and seeing the potential will become second nature. You'll know the right questions to ask in regards to making ready cost, occupancy, evictions, and other tenant related questions.

After the results of due diligence indicates a good deal, take a loan from the bank and acquire the real estate property. Rent the property and your tenants will pay the mortgage with surplus for yourself. You see, when you're in this position, Lenders will give you seventy to seventy five percent of the money needed to buy the property. With just about thirty percent, you're now the owner of the entire property. As soon as you can rent the property however, you no longer have to use your own money to pay the mortgage. This is a classic example of using debt to acquire wealth. Using debt or other people's money to acquire assets that produces cash flow is a mindset of the rich. Do not forsake this mindset.

In the example given above, the bank in essence is the master mind because they loan other people's money to serious credible people and institutions and collect an attractive interest while giving the depositors of money the absolute minimum in interest. We discussed the prospect of establishing a bank and this certainly would be one of the many benefits of it. Taking a loan to buy assets is like taking a play straight out of the bank's playbook. As I've mentioned over and over again, repeat all ventures that are substantially profitable. This strategy is clever and takes a life of its own as you continue to accelerate your wealth. The more asset acquisition you partake, the more your net worth grows, meaning bigger profits for you.

Other benefits of commercial real estate is appreciation. An investment in this type of property is certainly going to appreciate over time. If you decide to sell it after a few years, the value would have increased. The extent of the increase depends on comparable sales data for the area or sub-market as well as improvements made to the property. It is not far-fetched to buy a property, do some repairs, add improvements and increase the value by at least twenty five to fifty percent. Experienced investors in this field can identify properties with such upside as it is called. It is therefore very practical to make money during the rehab phase if carefully calculated.

When you decide to sell a commercial real estate property, you can buy a bigger one and all the taxes are deferred. It is called a 1031 exchange. This is an IRS code that allows an investor to acquire a more expensive property or one with more units after selling a previous one without paying taxes on it. There are a few rules that must be followed such as the time-frame between the sale and acquisition as well as the value between the two properties. This is important for building wealth because you want to avoid liabilities everywhere you can.

Apart from the appreciation of commercial real estate assets, there are many other important benefits. Among them are depreciation. It is expected that the property has a useful life of 27.5 years according to the IRS. Consequently, you'll lower your tax liability in the form of tax savings each year. We all understand that a property wears out over time and that depreciation translates to tax deductions.

After owning a cash producing property for a couple of years with an appreciation in value and equity, the entire process can be repeated. Members of your team especially your real estate agents and brokers are going to be constantly presenting properties to you. A good team will know what you like and therefore will filter through and only present what fits your style. When you find another deal that produces cash flow, has an up-side, and meet your requirements, you can buy and increase your assets.

The same strategies can be used to acquire other related commercial real estate properties such as office building and shopping strips etc. Be advised that each type is a little different and therefore the key to success is education. Immerse yourself in learning and due diligence before making a purchase in any real estate. As mentioned previously, start small and gain some experience before going big.

A must have investment is the acquisition of rental commercial real estate property such as apartment complex, office building, hotels, shopping mall, high rise building or storage building. Again a team would be needed to vet the details of the property, complete the deal and manage the property. In any case, if done properly with essential systems and processes previously discussed, your wealth will only continue to grow to delightful net worth. A yearly evaluation of your assets along with your team will let you know when to make the next move.

Commercial real estate is a great overall asset area for wealth building and the most stable of them all is apartment complexes. There are many benefits that come with real estate investments such as low out of pocket investments because most lenders will lend up to seventy five percent of the sale price. Think about it, the control and management of a multi-million dollar property and you only invest up to twenty five percent. Meanwhile the total cost of the project is credited to you since you own the mortgage. It opens greater doors and places you in other exclusive networks.

You will certainly enjoy appreciation as well as depreciation benefits. With appreciation, it is a natural thing that occurs with real estate due to economic factors. If trained properly however, you can acquire properties with an upside and instantly increase the appreciation by large amount. Let's say you buy a property that needs some improvement or upgrades. Get it done and increase rent on each unit. The raise in rent will cause your NOI to increase and therefore instant value appreciation. When this occurs, depreciation which is a tax deduction will increase as well because it is based on the value over a twenty seven years period. The improvement has to be cost effective so that there is a cash flow increase when the expenses are factored in.

You can even do a 1031 exchange when you buy a bigger or more expansive property without paying any taxes. The premise of doing this transaction is that you don't just sell the property. You sell to acquire another one. Usually you'll sell to acquire a bigger property or a more profitable property. Regardless of what you buy, it must be done within a specific amount of time and requirements. Among some of the guidelines are the same tax payer doing the swap and up to six months maximum time to complete. Tax is a liability and takes money out of your pocket. Money that can be invested into other assets so it is good to defer it through this exchange.

The most important of all the benefits of real estate investment is cash flow. When due diligence is done correctly, you can acquire a property that will affect your cash flow positively from the very first month after the deal is complete. Although, I've mentioned many benefits that can be enjoyed through commercial real estate, cash flow should be the motivator. It is immediate, on a monthly basis while the other benefits happens once a year. In fact, after reviewing the numbers and doing much due diligence, do not buy any property that is not already cash flow positive. Even when the opportunities are there, buy the ones with positive cash flow and let the areas of improvements be the icing on the cake.

Diversifying When it Makes Sense

Whether you engage in one business or a series of businesses, once you have reached a million dollar net worth, it's time to further diversify your wealth strategies. This does not mean a million dollars in the bank, just your worth in assets. When you are generating an attractive return, your first plan should be to expand or duplicate the entire process. Just think if you have a business with two hundred and fifty thousand dollars in profit yearly. Expanding three more times or establishing three more businesses just like it will put you at one million dollars in profit yearly. Expansion or duplication becomes easier every time because you've traveled that road before.

There are times when expansion is more logical than duplication and other times, the latter. For instance, a digital subscription service business should be expanded and not duplicated. After all, you create a product once and sell it over and over again on a monthly or yearly subscription. An example would be a membership website where subscribers are given a login access as long as they continue to pay their due subscription. Taking more customers after reaching a certain threshold only means bigger servers, database capability with more staff to handle customer service and technical issues. On the other hand you can only expand some services business so far before you max out. Examples would be private schools or a hospitals. In these cases your expansion really becomes duplication. I believe you get the idea.

Diversify your asset classes only when it makes sense to do so. There are many ways to do it. The hands free and easiest way to buy a piece of a company is through shares. If you have not engage in buying a piece of reputable and profitable publicly traded company in the form of paper stocks and bonds, you should consider it. As Always, you will have to go back to the drawing board and do the research before making the purchase. It's not difficult as all these companies have all the data you need right on their websites in the investor relations section. You can look at graphs and charts along with historic performances.

Typically the companies that shows a steady growth over ten years or more are a good place to start. You must however look at many other factors before making a decision to purchase its stocks and bonds. Once you gain some experience and become fluent, you can start looking into new companies and even startup ventures. More on this will also be covered later in this section.

In the pursuit for wealth creation, you have to master the art of acquiring more assets. After all, I've repeatedly stressed the fact that assets pay you money. Do not buy liability because you have to pay it. Securing money to fund additional businesses or ventures becomes easier when you have great credit and own a profitable business. Lenders see it as collateral and therefore assume a lower risk in funding you. You are even regarded as less risky when you have a track record of making timely payments on your previous loan as shown on your business credit report. The question of income becomes irrelevant since you determine your own income. Again, you are buying more assets but doing it with other investors or lenders money.

All your initial hard work will pay off in more ways than one. The bank will lend you money for all the items I listed in the wealth building basket of asset classes but do not borrow money to buy stocks and bonds. You see, although there are risk associated with all businesses and investments, stocks and bonds or paper assets and can be completely lost. This is not the case for businesses because the building, if you own it, the machinery, equipment, company vehicles, furniture, electronics and appliances and inventory can all be liquidated should the business shut down. The business itself can be sold if necessary. That is not the case for stocks therefore due to these and other circumstances, it is not wise to borrow for stocks and bonds purchase.

Investments for Portfolio Income

Another profitable way of owning parts or shares of other business is by participating in the stock market itself as opposed to buying shares directly from a company. It is a place where trading takes place between buyers and sellers. When it first began in the 16th century in Europe, all trading were done at a physical location called the stock exchange. Today there are many stock exchanges such as New York, London, Tokyo, Chicago, Shanghai and hundreds more, however with the emergence of the internet, most trading are now conducted electronically. You can literally sit in front of your computer, laptop, or even smartphone, set up an account online, make a deposit and begin trading. In fact, it has never been easier to buy or sell a stock.

When a company has done relatively well and wants to expand. Rather than using its own money for expansion or a loan, it may elect to sell some of its shares to raise the money. Before it can do such a thing, it must make a transition from a privately owned to a public owned company by filling documents with the security and exchange commission (SEC) in the United States or its equivalent in other countries. This act is called Initial public offering or IPO. The company will decide how many shares it's willing to sell and open it up to the stock market. The public, whether a person or an entity can now buy stocks or shares in that business entity making each buyer a part owner.

This is where you come in as an investor. People and institutions purchase stocks with the expectations that the value will increase over time. If it does, you can sell and make a profit. Stocks prices are forever changing due to market dictations and people are always buying and selling so a typical stock in the course of a day will fluctuate by the minute from opening to closing of the stock market. Before buying shares in any company however, there must be some research to make sure the company is financially sound, it has great leadership and vision and it has a steady history of growth and value. Intrinsic value is the actual value, not the market value of an asset or a company. To evaluate intrinsic value properly, you must fundamentally examine both qualitative and quantitative aspects. This means that you have to look at management and its model as well as the amount of cash flow it has. The subject of knowing how to read a financial statement is once again raised.

An investor will look at indicators such as price to earnings ratio or P/E, and previous paid dividends. As always, there's no substitute for education before you enter a new area of business. In addition education on the subject and working with a mentor that has had success in the stock market is highly advisable. Read publications like The Wall Street Journal and Investor's Business Daily. You can also learn the ins and outs of trading at Investopedia.com

There are many financial services institutions that work as intermediaries between the trader and the stock market. When you are ready to dive in, search for online discount brokers and look for ones that are well established with high ratings and low commission fees. Be sure to get a written disclosure of all fees before you sign up. Some of the top firms include Merrill Lynch, Charles Schwab, Fidelity, Vanguard and E-Trade. Vanguard is one of the largest investment companies in the world. It manages over 4.5 Trillion dollars in assets. All the above mentioned firms are very competitive and reputable.

Stocks and Bonds

As mentioned above, when you participate in the purchase of shares from a company, it is considered stocks or ownership stakes. It is not unusual for a company on the stock market to have millions or in some cases billions of owners. The percentages of ownership for most people are minuscule nonetheless it is ownership. When companies make profits, part of it can be declared as dividend and paid to the shareholders. This is one benefit of having equity in the company in which you purchased stocks. The other benefit is an increase in stock prices also known as capital gains.

Bonds on the other hand is simply debt. A company or a government can issue bonds, meaning debt that is promised to be paid at a future date. It is a loan that is borrowed from the public and certificates are issued to validate it. The certificate indicate a maturity date, interest rate and a dollar amount to be paid. Bond holder will receive their interest on their money a couple of times a year. At the maturity date, the original amount of money invested is returned to the bond holder. So in a nutshell, a bond holder will be paid interest as well as the original bond amount when it reached its maturity date.

Stocks and bonds are just two ways corporations use to raise capital. They use these funds to operate the business, expand or acquire other business. In most cases, they will pay you a higher interest than what a bank pays so people have more to gain from bonds than leaving their money in a savings account. The company at the same time enjoys paying less interest to bond holders than they would pay if they borrowed from a bank. As a result, it appears like a win for all parties.

Do keep in mind that as with any investment, you can lose everything if the company goes into default. Though rare, this can certainly happen.

The key is doing your research to make sure the company has solid financial statement and steady growth history as well as other crucial indicators. When you decide to make an investment of any kind, you should always consult with your financial adviser for his or her professional insight.

Financial statement

I have stressed the importance of having the ability to read and interpret financial records several times throughout this text. What exactly is a financial statement one might ask? It is a formal record that outlines the financial activities of an entity. It has three parts. They are income statement, balance sheet and statement of cash flow or retained earnings. Each one of these three documents has its purpose.

The income statement shows an overview of income and expenses for a period of time, usually a year. It breaks down the cost and expenses associated with the revenue and calculates earnings per share or EPS. You may have heard someone say, what is your bottom line? Well, you can find it at the bottom of an income statement. That is where gains or losses are revealed. The top shows gross or how much revenue was generated and then all the expenses are deducted as you work your way down. The cost of goods sold, operating expense and depreciation, interest and taxes are just a few items you'll see on the income statement. Whatever is left, whether profit or loss is your bottom line.

The balance sheet provides a snapshot of assets, liabilities an owner's equity or stockholders' equity. As I've mentioned a multitude of times, asset are things of value. They can be sold but most importantly they make you money. They are tangible and intangible such as physical properties and trademarks or patents. Liabilities are the amount of money the company owes to banks, landlord, suppliers, taxes, or simply bills. The remainder if all assets were sold and liabilities paid is called the owners' equity or stockholders' equity. In other words if the business as liquidated today, whatever is left will be shared by the shareholders.

The statement of cash flow brings it all together. They merge the income statement and the balance sheet to reveal operating, investing and financial activities of the company. This document captures the inbound and outbound of the money at a particular time. You should always have cash flow to pay bills and when necessary, purchase assets. The three areas that cash flow derives are operating, investing and financial activities. Below are examples of a financial statements

Balance Sheet Example

Equity			
Share capital	150 000	150 000	130 000
Share premium	232 343	232 343	32 925
Other reserves	6 735	6 834	7 119
Retained earnings	148 708	66 225	65 945
Net profit for the period	43 346	82 483	41 307
Total equity	**581 132**	**537 885**	**277 296**
Liabilities			
Non-current liabilities			
Long-term trade liabilities	-	864	2 470
Long-term bank loans	-	-	1 788
Finance lease liabilities	2 699	3 745	5 772
Long-term payables due to related parties	177 295	178 597	27 235
Deferred tax liabilities	-	-	539
	179 994	183 206	37 804
Current liabilities			
Short-term payables due to related parties	40 752	12 405	35 548
Short-term bank loans	3 636	24 680	9 137
Loans received	4 332	4 962	-

Trade payables	7 846	8 367	3 102
Finance lease liabilities	1 488	1 620	2 477
Tax liabilities	1 948	567	6
Payables to employees and social security institutions	61	58	554
Other liabilities	5 399	4 227	9 871
	65 462	**56 886**	**60 695**
Total liabilities	**245 456**	**240 092**	**98 499**
Total equity and liabilities	**826 588**	**777 977**	**375 795**

Income Statements Example

Gains from transactions with financial instruments	36 121	49 168
Losses from transactions with financial instruments	(1 109)	(6 588)
Net profit from transactions with financial instruments	**35 012**	**42 580**
Interest income	10 582	7
Interest expense	(2 132)	(933)
Net profit/ (loss) from interest	**8 450**	**(926)**
Gains from foreign exchange differences	578	279
Losses from foreign exchange differences	(16)	(5)
Net profit from foreign exchange differences	**562**	**274**
Other financial income/ (losses), net	**592**	**(75)**
Operating income	3 883	2 982

Operating expenses	(3 325)	(3 528)
Operating result	**558**	**(546)**
Profit for the period before tax	**45 174**	**41 307**
Tax expense, net	(1 828)	-
Net profit for the period	**43 346**	**41 307**

Statement of Cash Flows Example

Cash flow from operating activities		
Proceeds from short-term loans	33 781	39 738
Payments for short-term loans	(24 332)	(46 560)
Proceeds from sale of short-term financial assets	37 717	49
Receipts from customers	4 493	6 882
Payments to suppliers	(6 760)	(2 950)
Interest receipts	-	7
Payments to employees and social security institutions	(385)	(278)
Taxes paid	(454)	(1 926)
Other cash flows from operating activities	-	(2)
Net cash flows from operating activities	**44 060**	**(5 040)**
Investment activities		
Purchase of non-current assets	(8 260)	(25 016)
Proceeds from sale of non-current financial assets	16 326	41 195
Purchase of investments in subsidiaries and associates	(27 636)	(31 950)
Long-term loans granted	(9 022)	-
Net cash flows from investing activities	**(28 592)**	**(15 771)**
Financing activities		
Long-term loans received	18 497	38 991
Repayments of long-term and bank loans received	(39 682)	(12 401)
Discharge of finance lease liabilities	(1 178)	(1 133)
Interest paid	(860)	(589)

Net cash flows from financing activities	(23 223)	24 868
Gains from foreign exchange differences	563	6
Cash and cash equivalents, beginning of period	92 845	26 392
Net (decrease)/ increase of cash and cash equivalents	(7 192)	4 063
Cash and cash equivalents, end of period	85 653	30 455

Generally accepted accounting principles or GAAP is a standard that is recognized worldwide to ensure continuity of information across the globe. It is very important that all persons that aspire to own or operate a business learns how to read and interpret a financial statement. Your CPA should go through your financial statements with you annually.

It is understood that we all must have a home and transportation. When you buy a big home and drive a nice car, always remember that money could have been used to buy more assets. Until you reach your goal of becoming wealthy, live moderately and practice a modest lifestyle. The discipline required is same as the one needed when you first begin other task. It starts off seemingly difficult but gets easier with time.

Bitcoin and ICO's

There's a new virtual currency being spent worldwide and it is called Bitcoin. A crypto-currency, Bitcoin is a technology and also a medium of exchange. Its platform is solely decentralized. The exchanges occur through peer to peer with no bank or financial institution acting as a hub or central control. The technology was created by an anonymous group or person by the name of Satoshi Nakamoto in 2009. Prior in 2008, Satoshi Nakamoto released the white paper to his mailing list calling it bitcoin and describing it as a peer to peer digital currency and an electronic cash system. It was developed on a Blockchain technology and was the first to find a solution to the problem of double spending for digital currency.

Satoshi Nakamoto released the Bitcoin software version 0.1 and the first units of Bitcoins. The technology is based on cryptography and subsequent bitcoins are created through a process called mining. All transaction takes place after proof of work has been verified. The people who create Bitcoins and verifies proof of work are called miners. The process is accomplished through a complex mathematical data. It is by nature, time consuming and very costly. Super-fast computers that uses excessive electricity and generates lots of heat are used to do the mining. As a result, large fans and air condition are installed to protect the computers from overheating and burning up.

Consensus by the miners are permanently recorded and cannot be changed. Blockchain technology enables each consensus to be embedded on a chain of blocks and more blocks are added each time there's a new transaction. Since its inception, bitcoin has nearly reached twenty thousand dollars per bitcoin. It occurred in December 2017. The market for cryptocurrencies are highly volatile and at the time of this writing, the price for one bitcoin was around eight thousand dollars. This is still remarkable, since the very first notable indirect transaction was 2 pizzas from Papa Johns for ten thousand Bitcoins.

The technology is an open source therefore other programmers and computer science techs can build onto it. As a result, thousands of variations of the technology is being developed with each having its own name and function. Arguably, the second most popular cryptocurrency is Ethereum. It has its own functions and many firms uses its platform for their own crypto technology.

So why should you care about bitcoins? Well, for starters, it reached a market cap of eight hundred and thirty five billion dollars during its highest peak in December 2017. Though it has lost one hundred and seventy billion dollars since, it is still number one among all the cryptocurrencies and is expected a continued growth over time. Many other forms of cryptocurrencies in general are emerging each day merchants such as Overstock.com, virgin airlines and subway to name a few are already accepting Bitcoins as a form of payment. There's currently not much regulation because it's new but that will change with time. In December 2017, United States commodity futures trading commission (CFTC) announced that financial firms Chicago (CME) and Chicago (CBOE) will begin Bitcoin future trading

To buy Bitcoin itself, you can simply go to a crypto-currency exchange website. They'll issue you a code to access your Bitcoin that you can then store in an electronic wallet. You can also store it on the exchange itself or on a hard wallet. A hard wallet is the most secured means since only you have access to it and it can never be hacked. Once you buy Bitcoin, you can then spend it, trade it or sell it without going through a third party. For beginners, it may be best to use an exchange to buy, sell and trade to avoid scams. The most popular exchanges have been around for a number of years and have strict requirements such as identification verification and bank or credit card information.

Initial coin offering or ICO is when a crypto-currency or token company as it is sometimes called first goes public. I mentioned earlier that there are hundreds of companies emerging each day with their own crypto-currency. These companies will eventually do an ICO launch and get on an exchange for public trading. Before they do it, they tend to have a pre-sale to raise money. This practice is similar to what regular stock market companies do with venture capitalist by giving them a chance to get in before the public. Since this technology is new and unregulated, these pre-ICO's are offered to the general public. Those that get in early can gain a lot when it goes public. That said, Bitcoins are still high volatile and therefore investors must do their own due diligence before acquiring bitcoins. Failure to do your research could result in a big loss.

The key as an investor is to do your research and see if the company and its product is solid. There are many indicators that can be used to analyze it, such as the team behind the firm. What experience do they have? Does the company have a prototype? What is the price point, the market capitalization and price per token? What problem they are solving and ultimately how much money they need and how much have already been raised?

You can also check with some of the ICO rating companies that uses complex metrics to evaluate ICO's. As with all ventures and investments, do your due diligence. There is no substitute for research and be sure to consult your financial adviser before making any investments. There is much that can be gained in ICO and pre- ICO however, you can also lose it all due to the extreme volatility.

Section III

TRANSGENERATIONAL WEALTH

&

GIVING BACK

CHAPTER SIX

Diversify Asset Classes Using More Debt

Diversification means multiple streams of

Income from a variety of assets

Conduct Scheduled Evaluations

It is necessary to do a yearly evaluation to see how your business is performing. There are so many reasons why a business may choose to expand. The first sign to look for when considering expansion is demand and load. When demand becomes greater than supply and load makes it mandatory to impose overtime on your staff, it's time to consider expansion. A coffee shop that continues to have long lines may expand to provide faster service and make room for more customers.

After three consecutive years of positive cash and substantial profitability, you can make a sound judgment that your systems are working and therefore you can actually expand. In such cases, you have formulated a wining system and therefore it's alright to duplicate that formula. A ROI may be used to make such a determination. Be sure to pay attention to the size of the profit or business. For example ten percent gain is relative to a specific dollar amount.

Expansion in itself takes many forms. Some may require more employees as in a case where the demand is too great to meet without making your staff work more than eight hours a day. Occasional overtime is fine but when it becomes a routine, expansion is the way out. After all, all overtime hours are paid at a rate of one and half times. This means someone that makes fourteen dollars an hour now makes twenty one dollars an hour once they reach overtime.

Imagine if you have a staff of just five all being paid at one and half times on a regular bases. Your operating cost will increase significantly. This issue can easily be resolved with a couple of addition staff. They will be paid at entry level which in most cases is less than what current employees earn. If these employee are not needed on a full time basis, their schedule can easily be adjusted to accommodate the needs of the business.

A business that stocks inventory may reach a point where their product selection growth dictate an expansion in physical size. Think of a retailer of medical supplies for an example. The store may be five thousand square feet of space, Let's say the store sells convalescent items, incontinent items, ambulatory items, diagnostic items, personal care items, respiratory items, manual mobility items, power mobility items, and medical uniforms. With these items, the store is filled to capacity. Then a year later a new hospital or nursing home is built next door.

That single act will cause the demand of additional supplies such as hospital beds and furnishings as well as patient transfer equipment like trapeze and patient lift. Surely these items will require additional space in order to stock them. Not doing this will force your customers to go elsewhere. For the sake of convenience, customers will buy the rest of the items at the other place as opposed to going to two different places. Not paying attention to these types of changes can be detrimental to your business. Yet a child care service that is licensed for two hundred and forty children with a ten thousand square foot facility in a retail strip may expand differently. They may either buy a land near the original location and build a bigger facility with rooms for expansion or get a second location nearby. Although proximity is important to parents, if the center provides excellent service to their children, they may disregard the inconvenience for comfortability as long as it is not too far. Not analyzing the growth properly could cost a lot of money. In this example, if the business owner is leasing the space, it would be wise to buy or build its own. If the business is not very profitable at full capacity, then the business owner must activate its exit strategy.

If your capacity to reach people is limited by a certain number of miles radius due to customers having other options or just not willing to do the additional commuting, and the business is doing well, open another location. This type of expansion execution can lead to franchising of your business. There's nothing easier than selling processes that you have already created for a fee plus royalties. Sure, you will have to provide training and support but with a smart system, this can be done with minimum effort.

You see, different circumstances calls for different action plan but the worse that a business can do is ignore changes, in this cases expansion when it is vital for the continued success of the company. As you can see, some expansions are human resources issue, some are physical space issue, some are product and services issue, and some are additional location type of expansion. The idea is to accommodate the most effective, yet least expensive method. In the case of a second location, the idea of a franchise in the making begins to develop.

A lot of individuals would want to know, when do you liquidate a business? Well, you may liquidate as a last option. Carefully monitoring your business could reveal signs that could lead a company to sell. Selling is always a better option even if it is sold at a discount due to lack of performance. The buyer may have processes already in place to turn the business around.

Just because one owner couldn't navigate the business to success does not mean the business is doomed. Often at times, the lack of systems that addresses managerial, marketing, and operational among others, causes a company to fail. With leadership that have experience and clear direction, a company can be acquired and turned around within a short time. Investors that acquire failing business usually have systems in place before they consider buying such businesses.

When your business is insolvent or no longer able to pay its bills when they become due, it's time to liquidate. It is not smart to sink further into debt by trying to sustain a failing business. The only exception is having a proven system, different from the previous that is being instituted. In that scenario, a timeline for improvement must be defined and if none is seen, proceed with the exit strategy.

Remember, anytime a business chooses to liquidate, there must be an assessment of who is owed and in what manner. For instance, your lender has interest in your business assets and must be informed. The business accountant and lawyer can also help with the process. Depending on the extent of the debt, it may be necessary to file for bankruptcy. Again such things will require an attorney and account to ensure it is done correctly.

From time to time, you'll see a major company going through store closings and liquidation. From furniture stores to electronics, grocery to retails, regardless of the sector, not being financially sound will lead to a business's demise. A good reason why consulting is a great idea if you don't have any experience. It helps with systems and processes that will ensure success and longevity.

During liquidation, some businesses will sell its inventory at marked down prices and continue this way until all items are sold. This method works well when staff and management are in place. Others do their liquidation by auctioning their items. Whether it is sold in bundles or individually often depends on the type of items. In some cases, the lender may take charge of the liquidation process to ensure they get as much of their money back as possible. Most lenders have contracts with auction companies to handle their needs.

Diversifying Your Asset Classes

All through this text, I have emphasized the need to repeat what's working well in terms of substantial profit. My rule of thumb is twenty five percent of every one million dollar, however that number is totally dependent on the type of investment. You have to look at factors that are important to you such as opportunity cost. This is where the diversification of asset classes comes into play. Let's say you are now the owners of a few successful businesses, a few commercial real estate properties and a few thousand shares of some high performing stocks. You also have a couple of million dollars of life insurance as well as a side note. These assets will continue to produce cash on demand an make you very wealthy. This will be explained further in the Trans generational wealth section.

In the spirit of diversification, a few successful businesses means several businesses in different market areas. For instance, two or more restaurants, dry cleaners, gas stations/convenient stores, retail shops, private schools, merchant and surveillance services, postal services, electronics/phone repair shop, home remodeling and so on. By the way, any of these businesses should be structured so its daily operation does not require your presence. The key to success is hiring the best people and treating them exceptionally well while removing anyone that fails to meet their duties on a continuous basis.

The same applies to commercial real estate properties. A few mid-size residential apartment units, office suites, retail and shopping centers and storage units. I tend to stay away from single family units unless there is much to gain in either wholesaling or rehabbing to flip or rent. In that case be sure to determine the purpose before pursuing the property. If you're making repairs to sell, also known as fix and flip, you'll need a good estimate of repair cost and factor it in the sale price. The sale price must be well below market value. Rental on the other hand, a quick rule of thumb is half of the rental price should cover the mortgage and expenses such as property tax, insurance, maintenance/repairs, HOA fees, and management fees.

Own Assets in Different Sectors of the Economy

Likewise, your paper assets must also be well diversified. Scientifically speaking, you'll want to cover several of the 10 sectors of the economy. You may invest in all areas but you should not form a habit of let's say NIKE is doing well so all the investment goes into it. Yes, it is an apparel company so investment should not remain in similar companies. Instead spread it out to reach energy, healthcare, utilities, telecom, materials, information technology, financial, consumer discretionary and consumer staples. This strategy will help create a balance so in the event that one or two sectors are experiencing market correction or hardship, the others stay on track.

You are now definite that all of your assets are doing well, it is time to look into buying an oil drilling or mineral mining company, a financial institution like a bank, an insurance company, a solar energy company, a media and content company. Inquire these asset classes in any order you please. They are all the next logical step as you extend your level of diversification and fool proof your wealth to outlive you and a number of other generations in your family tree.

Looking at some high risk but extremely high return investment such as oil and mineral mining, you'll have to partner with experienced people with great track record. The key to being successful in these areas is networking with people that have a proven record of profiting in these industries but be sure to do due diligence until you've exhausted all areas of data. A mining or oil project may take years without finding anything but when they do, you will gain high returns than that of any other investments. For instance, investing in the oil business offshore can take you to the next level of wealth beyond your wildest dreams. It is not unusual to earn upward of three hundred percent interest on these types of investment.

Opening a bank is the very essence of your money making money. You can start with a minimum of five hundred thousand dollars and show a capital of ten million dollars. Upon passing an FBI background check, having a few experience bankers on board, and meeting a few other requirements, you are in. Banks are allowed to create and extend credit before even looking for deposit to substantiate it. They are also backed by the central banks that can create reserves when they feel like it. When I say create reserve, I mean print money. If you have no experience in banking and finance, you'll have to partner with some talented bankers to make it work.

Another major business for attaining great wealth is selling insurance. Having a capital of two hundred and fifty thousand dollars to one million will get you started. You must have a sound business plan and meet insurance carriers' requirements and minimum sales quota. There are many forms of insurance coverage with each carrying its own risk. Some of the more common ones are Life, Auto, and Homeowners. Each carries its own level of risk. You make money when there are no losses or minimum losses. You can also lose a tremendous amount in major loss cases. Careful planning by experience agents is key to ensuring you have sufficient fund and to avoid bankruptcy when there are major losses.

Joining a major agency and learning the basics and or partnering with an experience agent is advisable. Either way, someone from your company has to be a licensed agent. It is very important to structure your company correctly for maximum protection. Once you get your tax id number from the IRS and purchase errors and omission insurance, you can register with your state. It varies by state but you'll certainly need permits and licenses to operate. Be sure to get a good agency management system.

With your multitude of businesses in the black collectively, a few hundred of commercial real estate units producing cash flow, a substantial amount of paper assets doing well, perhaps you can take a bit more calculated risk and participate in hedge funds. You and your team should be sophisticated investors at this point so it's logical to enter this territory.

A hedge fund as stated is limited to sophisticated investors and institutions. It is not regulated by the United States Security and Exchange Commission (SEC), as is the case with mutual funds. It is a high risk, high reward venture, unlike mutual funds. These investors form a partnership and invest using borrowed money. Again, due to its high risk factor, players must be accredited and have a net worth of at least one million in addition to having significant knowledge in investing.

At this point, you own several businesses and several investments properties. Your team is fired up, your net worth is rising, the question becomes, what's next. There are no shortage of assets but now you want to be a little more aggressive. You already own a variety of assets classes that has equity and produces cash flow. Perhaps you can sort after higher returns. Through networking, you can find development deals that can meet your desire.

A higher reward and higher risk investment known as private equity funds can be considered. This type usually deals with startup companies and development deals. A shopping mall project, a medical complex or perhaps a chain of hotels are all viable development deals. It must be noted that both the hedge funds and the private equity funds are not as liquid as mutual funds so you can be locked in for several years without the ability to sell your shares.

Safeguard What You Have Built

As soon as you reach a certain level of wealth, trans-generational wealth has to become a priority. It is simply wealth systems that continue to grow through multiple generations. Talking to your family about your plans and wishes ahead of time will enhance the chances of continued legacy. Make sure they understand your assets and how it is to outlive you, the next generation and many more to come. For these reasons, they must be very familiar with your institutions, life insurance policies, other assets and its protective mechanisms already in place.

The first thing that comes to mind in terms of wealth systems for trans generational wealth is SFO's or single family offices. It is a private company that manages family wealth from one hundred million and beyond. They will assist with investment and trusts strategy and managing the managers of your various companies. Apart from managing the wealth, they handle many other things like set benchmarks and evaluate them for accountability. They will handle all your philanthropy as well but again, its primary function is the centralization of the wealth and its sub managers.

Do not bother with SFO's if you have not reach the wealth status mentioned above as it cost around one million a year for them to take over your affairs. Even if your net worth had not reach this hundred million threshold, through sound investment practices, they're sure to get there by the next generation. This is why is so important that your family know and understand your intention by this time, trans-generational wealth.

Your Estate should be an institution so whether you are here or not, it should continue to operate. With sound policies and proper management, the wealth is sure to cross many generations to come. You have done your part when your organization owns and control a sizable portion of the total wealth on Earth. Remember to enjoy life throughout the process of wealth building. Do not forsake family and friends for the sake of building wealth. Instead, have a logical balance that include time sharing engagements in matters of your social life and wealth creation.

CHAPTER SEVEN

Asset Protection

Protect everything that has sufficient value to your organization

Why Asset Protection is a Must

There should not be any more convincing needed on the subject of asset protection. Throughout this book, I have iterated the importance of protecting things that have value to you. Examples have been given and scenarios illustrated. If you still need convincing, here it is. Things happen. When they do, it is better to have prepared for them than to be caught off guard. There's no warning because no one can read the future. We do know however that there are cycles of history that repeats itself over time. We also know that our human race is not perfect so mistakes are made yet forgiveness seems rare.

You lock your doors at home because you don't want thieves to steal your belongings. The same concept applies when it comes to protecting your assets. It should not be left up for grabs. Asset protection is fundamental to wealth building and gives you peace of mind. Protect yourself at all times by taking essential measures whenever necessary as you continue to create a legacy of wealth. Build the kind of wealth that never dies. Let it outlive you, your children, your grandchildren and their decedents. You do it by constructing asset protection beyond your life.

Specialized Attorney

Now that you've built institutions, you must protect it and ensure that it outlives you. To do it, the first thing would be to sit with a reputable attorney who specializes in asset protection and estate planning that governs the home of your institutions. The consultation should address all your assets and how to best protect it from theft, lawsuits, probate, excessive tax, and lastly anything that you have not thought about. Specialize attorney in the field of asset protection know how to best protect everything you and your organization owns.

Most people know about personal identity theft but there's also business identity theft. Protect yourself and your entities against both. Thieves look for weak or poorly protected people and businesses to target. When this occurs, a large quantity of money can be stolen, as well as business credit and products can be ordered and invoiced in the victim or it's company's name. You must guard against these potential illegal activities so it never happens to you. Protection at times also serve as a deterrent against such vultures.

It seems a lot of people want the smallest opportunity to sue a prosperous company. These days, issues that can easily be resolved outside of litigation are taken to court in hopes of winning a substantial judgment. Avoid being the defendant in such cases by protecting your assets. Taking measures to protect yourself properly means that you become more untouchable than many others. If your assets have layers of protection, it makes it difficult for attorneys to go after you.

They want cases that are seen as easy to win and substantial amounts gained.

When a would-be plaintiff consults an attorney, that attorney will conduct an asset search. They do this primarily to decide whether to take the case or not especially if being paid is contingent on winning the case. Asset searches can reveal a lot and if they found assets that are not protected correctly, they will go after it. If documents are not properly filed etc. the courts can pierce the corporate veil and regard you and your entity as one. Don't give them this opportunity over your hard work. If your assets are properly protected, they will not waste their time.

Insurances

Do all you can to protect virtually all your personal assets as well as business assets adequately. Although it's never too late to implement protection over your assets, it should start the minute you begin to acquire assets. If it has significant value, it should be protected in some way. For instance, a home owner needs insurance to cover damages of the home as well as the content inside the home and any structures on the property. The same applies to a commercial building owner. It too must be protected from the same type of losses.

Natural disaster damages as a result of Tornado, Hurricane, Flood and other natural disasters and even fire and vandalism should be covered. Insure the property adequately and keep a low deductible if at all feasible. All vehicles of significant value must also have comprehensive coverage. I'm talking about all personal as well as company's vehicles and other machinery.

The protections mentioned above are strictly for loss or damage. Your assets must also be protected from lawsuits and unnecessary taxes as well. Many states have homestead laws that prevents being forced to sell and settle or lien being placed on your property as a result of court judgment. If your state has no such protection, then your personal property should be protected through a land trust etc.

As for your business assets, each business should have its own independent protection. For most businesses, the first line of defense is general liability insurance. This type of insurance will in most cases take care of any lawsuits without losing any assets within the business. In this litigious society however, the plaintiff attorney may attempt to go beyond the insurance by suing for more than the dollar amount of insurance coverage.

Corporations

To protect your business against an act of greed, your business needs a second line of defense. Properly forming an entity such as a corporation, a limited liability company or limited partnership will be your second tier protection. Doing this ensures that no one can go beyond the assets within this entity. Each of the various formations mentioned above has its purpose. Your business attorney and tax adviser can guide you as to which is appropriate for the type of business you conduct.

Any one of them is better than none at all. We don't build businesses and allow others to take advantage of it. We build businesses that outlives us and is then passed on to our families. A thriving company with all its protective mechanism already in place defines this philosophy. It should be a mentality of natural reflexes or habit. Just as most people put on their seat belt when they get in their cars, people should incorporate their business when they establish it. You'll enjoy other benefits of incorporating as well.

If your business is one that has a high risk of litigation due to its nature, then yet a third line of protection will act as a deterrent against lawsuits. This line of protection can include strategies such as equity stripping or anonymity with a registered agent. Equity stripping is the action of withdrawing your equity out of your home every few years. This act is a turn off for attorneys who work on contingency. In other words they don't see much that they can go after. Anonymity makes it impossible for attorneys to see what you own. This is a case of out of sight, out of mind.

The extent to which you go in protecting what you've built varies from entity to entity and your competent attorney in asset protection will be the best person to advise you legally. In fact there are many more layers of strategies that can be implemented to protect your assets, so any potential predator would change their mind, when they realize there's nothing to gain by going after you.

Living Trust

It does not make sense to do a Will or a Living Will as some call it. Instead, talk to your attorney about establishing a Living Trusts as this document will save your family, time and money in the event of your demise. There will be no probate court which can take 6 months to a year and cost lots of money. Your love ones should focus on other things like properly grieving and reminiscing about the great times, not spending their time in court and wasting their inheritance on attorney fees and unnecessary taxes.

Avoid double taxation of your estate by creating a trusts as no tax is deducted on the principal because money entered into the trust is pre-taxed. The one thing you don't want is to build something for your family to inherit and minimize it by failure to plan properly. Although the 2017 United States Tax Plan has abolished estate tax, it may be reversed by another president in the future. Your lawyer will know the most current laws surrounding your estate in your area. Most likely, after adding your assets such as life insurance, businesses, stocks and properties, you'll exceed the threshold of not being taxed. It is therefore important that this aspect is protected as well.

It would be a shame to acquire wealth and lack the ability to protect it. Again, it is essential that you spend the money and have an experience attorney that specializes in asset protection review your unique circumstances. Such attorney can design documents to properly structure entities to minimize liability while maximizing anonymity. When correctly executed, your asset protection documents will insulate you from our litigious society.

This is what it's all about. Taking measures to ensure that your wealth successfully transfer to your family privately and without probate, other litigation or excessive tax. Even your other assets such as 401K, Roth IRA, Life insurance and others can all be poured into your living trusts in the event of your demise. By the way, the Roth IRA for your kids can be a partner in one of your real estate LLC and enjoy additional tax benefits but only when the money is used later for college or retirement. If you don't have such intentions, it would not be advantageous to partner your Roth IRA with real estate. Again there's no one size fits all for these types of protection so you must sit down with an experience lawyer and tax adviser in this field and have them custom design protection for your wealth.

Many in the personal finance sector understand that wealth strategies are based on individual goals and therefore cannot say with one hundred percent certainty about what one must do to build wealth. I'm no different however with all things considered such as arbitrage, opportunity cost, ROI, appreciation, depreciation, proper management, dividends, 1031 exchange, lawsuits, identity theft, and leverage, I can certainly say that the process outlined throughout this book is surely among the best ways of becoming and staying rich forever.

I can also say that if careful and strategic measures are not taken to protect ones assets, it can all vanish within a short period of time. It is therefore smart with the help of your team to formulate a system that protects your assets well beyond your own life and the next few generations to come. Some strategies may be a result of local laws and regulations which most likely differs from state to state and province to province. There are no substitute to assimilating a team that supports and work to push your agenda. These people must be compensated for their time and efforts and treated like valuable members.

Giving Back the Effective Way

Pay it forward by extending some effective assistance to those less fortunate. This subject is near and dear to my heart as you know from reading this book that a lady at a local bakery gave me a chance to sell bread on consignment when I was only nine years old in Ghana. That single act sparked the entrepreneurship in me and I haven't stopped ever since. Although this kind lady is no longer with us, in a way she made it possible for me to believe in my ideas.

Life is what you make it after you get the assistance you need. Metaphorically, I've never met a person that stands tall without standing on the shoulders of others. When you open your heart and help people, you have in essence helped many more than you would ever know. There are so many ways to help others and although there's no wrong way, take measures to make sure its effective.

Clean water, nutritious food, shelter, health, mental health, medicine, assistive devices, sanitation, clothes/shoes, public safety, respect, education, training, jobs, public transportation, opportunities, fairness, police protection, love, peace, advancement, choice, privacy and other human rights are just a few area that we as the human family can do a lot better in sharing. Just pick one and serve people in that arena. We must adopt "when one hurt, we all hurt" mentality because it's the right thing to do.

The data on how many people on this earth lack access to clean and safe drinking water will bring sadness to your heart. It is over one billion worldwide, yet next to air, water is the most abundant natural resource we have. The benefits of having a water solution everywhere is the promotion of sanitation, elimination of waterborne illness, and senseless time wasted on commuting great distances just to get water. Some water sources are contaminated while others are inaccessible. I am quite sure that the people will do the work, all that is needed is the hardware to make it possible.

Back to the basics with agriculture is one answer to nutritious food for all. We must grow food responsibly and locally on fertile grounds everywhere. Private unused land can be leased and cultivated to produce whole natural foods. When we eat better, we think better and consequently we are able to be better in our interactions with one another. Many people all over the globe lack basic nutrients found in natural foods. It can all be addressed one area at a time by fortunate people of the world. Success is much sweeter with a compassionate heart.

The shelter solution is compulsory next to food, water and clothing. Even considering the extreme heat and cold temperatures that many places encounter, it's plain to see that this issue deserves the attention of the fortunate. For those that are well of, no family member of yours should be homeless. When charity begins at home, it will definitely spread to other places. One area of real estate investment is to cater to section eight housing or its equivalent in other places. This is basically a government subsidized housing so most of the rent is paid by the government for lower income families. Another area could be flats or apartments building supplies donated to people to build a habitat for their families.

It is a fact that great health and mental health derives from eating natural foods and avoiding fake foods. People who live and eat naturally will not have much need for medicine. The challenge is starting and remaining consistent with diet. That said, there are many that need medicine for a host of medical issues. Partnering with pharmaceutical companies to create a generic version of their brand products will lower cost therefore becoming more accessible to an ordinary person.

Again prevention is better than cure so educating people on the importance of eating properly will save them from the dependence on medicine in many cases.

A simple hub where people can donate medical assistive devices of their love ones when they move to the other side will help many in need of such devices. These hubs, if strategically placed in cities around the world can serve as distribution centers to many other charity organizations that can get them to the patient. It can also welcome families to pick up directly. When the items in working order are no longer needed, they could be returned and made ready for the next patient.

Clothing and shoes factories all over the world throw away their so called defects. These items are in many cases very small discrepancies. Why not form a charity that negotiate the release of these items to help the less fortunate instead of throwing them away. All they have to do is remove their brand off the item so it does not appear as though their products are less than top quality. Certain things require a bit of persuasion but it's a small task for this level of humanitarianism.

The question of public safety is mostly the responsibility of the government. They collect taxes and part of that funds should be used for first responder institutions such as ambulance services, fire stations services and police. Yet, it is also beneficial when we all act as Good Samaritans, stay vigilant and report unusual things to the appropriate authorities. A step further would be volunteering your spare time to any of these services.

It feels good to be respected. No one should be so desensitized that they don't give or expect respect. Society as a whole does well when we have respect for one another. These values can only be taught at home as the media will teach you otherwise. Develop a principle of respect and double it for our elders. A rule of thumb is that people in your parents' age group are your elders. Give them extra respect and listen to them as the wisdom they disburse cannot be purchase with money. This charity does not cost a thing.

Education, training and jobs are all related. It can be formal or informal, however it is needed to create or to get a job. Take a few apprentice in your establishment and train them to also become business oriented. This act of paying it forward continues the cycle and creates more innovators to help advance our world. Do not limit your assistance to only your local geographical area. Instead travel and look for opportunities where you can expand your businesses while providing the education, training and jobs to that areas' demographics.

Look for areas where public transportation is not available but needed and contract with the government to fill these gaps buy providing services at a low cost to the public. It can be a network similar to Uber and Lift but paid primarily by the government since that's a responsibility of theirs anyway. More people will work when they have transportation and the economy benefits as a result. When people work, they spend money and some of that money may come directly to your business.

There are many people that have the desire to excel in life. These people tend to display their character in even the smallest things. If given an opportunity, many will exceed our expectations. People with such quality are an asset to a company but no one will ever know if they're not given a chance. The cost of not ensuring that the majority of people have opportunity is collectively slow advancement of humanity.

Fairness is when all are treated just and discrimination cease to exist. It is something that often gets overlooked mainly because many people don't truly understand it. Whether it's the workplace, marketplace, public venues, or at home, we must all exercise fairness. The end result would be police protection for all, love and peace in this world, and advancement in our individual prospective fields.

People should always have a choice in life. A certain belief should not be imposed on others without regard. Their privacy should not be invaded and dignity must be restored to all. Choice and privacy are basic human rights. The world can use plenty more organizations that advocate for these basic human rights.

I believe that when you've managed to be financially successful, it's nothing to establish a charitable organization to serve in the capacity of helping in areas of which you're most compassionate. We all have unique things that we care about as well as things that makes us feel sympathetic. Identify yours and provide assistance that makes a measurable difference.

Here are some ideas to get you started in determining how you can be of service to others. The first charity I want to address pertain to children. There are an estimated sixteen million children that struggle with hunger every day in the United States. This one is so shameful because it can easily be solved by re-routing all the food that is wasted each and every day. A charity organization with chapters in every city and sub-chapters in rural areas where families are incentivized to deliver nutritious food to registered children and their families would reduce this number significantly.

There is an estimated 1.3 billion people in Africa. It is a fact that's over half of its population live on less than two dollars a day. A charity organization that researches and educates businesses on how opening branches in cities across countries in Africa would benefit them in terms of cost, as well as eradicate poverty tremendously. This charity organization would illustrate how employing the local people and paying fair wages would create a better world while reducing operating cost by a large margin.

Many companies in Europe and America outsource their work to the people in Asia. It cuts down cost and the local people benefit from it however, the working conditions has many challenges from exceedingly long hours to low wages. A charity organization that serves as a watchdog to ensure these people are treated with dignity, worked reasonable hours and paid fairly would raise the morale of the local workers and ultimately productivity.

In these same places as well as the rest of the world, you will find gifted and talented young people with no opportunities to develop their ideas. Consequently, their vision of a better world fails to be realized. A Free academy in every state, country, or province that accepts children with exceptional display of academic achievement would innovate our world and push us into a more advance society collectively. This humanitarian acts will be copied and re-created by the very people that it benefited by reaching more and more people.

Our elders spend their last years in nursing homes with very little family visits and interactions. We must simply do better. Since parents and guardians took care of their children when there were unable to take care of themselves, the law of reciprocity should take place. An organization that encourages families to provide home comfort for their elders during their last days will clear a lot of conscience of people that would otherwise regret their decision of parents or guardian abandonment.

In fact all of the ideas above are not limited to one geographical area or demographics. The ideas can be implemented interchangeably so long as the need is there. We have been blessed with self-awareness, all our faculties, and ability to think, reason, and create all types of things to make life easier and enjoyable. We naturally feel good when we lend a helping hand. I'm confident that we will do more.

The troubles of this world are so massive that volumes after volumes of book could be written about it. No one can solve them all but the idea is for everyone to do what they can in the best way possible. I saw a video of the wild. In it, a small deer or gazelle was lost and was spotted by some hyenas. Just when they were ready to attack, a lion came out of nowhere and prevented it.

If a lion can protect a small animal from being eaten in the wild, and by the way the lion would have done the same for a small child, a human being can do miracles with just a little effort. We cannot let animals outdo humans in matters of care.

Conclusion

You now have in your hands something special that majority of the world doesn't and even worse, those that do will not take action on it. It is because people that fail to act have not realized that what they thought was difficult is actually very easy. They never knew because no effort was taken on their behalf. You are however an exception because you've not only purchased this book but you've actually read it all the way through. What this translates to me is that you are a person that can make a commitment and that is essential in the quest to acquire any level of wealth. Secondly you are displaying heavy traits of motivation and that too is an essential part of becoming independently wealthy. Lastly you have not only invested in Little Money Big Credit, but you've lend the time necessary to absorbed this fundamental knowledge all successful people already know.

Let me conclude by first sharing this ancient Chinese proverb with you;

"A journey of a thousand miles begins with a single step" Lao Tzu

If you have the will to succeed, you will. There are no excuses, only preparation. Plot on exactly what it is that you want to achieve and ensure that your every move is a calculated step towards that goal. You will be triumphant.

There's at least 7.5 Billion people in the world and half of this global population lives in poverty. Although the conditions surrounding this phenomenon varies, it is my personal belief that much of it can be eradicated. Imagine if the 33 million millionaires in the world today all made a sincere contribution towards a system that is designed specifically to permanently elevate people from such conditions. The result will be a brighter future for all mankind. Humans are blessed with extra ordinary capabilities and we should use it for uplifting each other's collectively without any regards to discrimination of any sort. Success is much more gratifying when helping others is built into your system.

For starters, inform others about this book when you have completed reading it. Doing this will enable others to also come in contact with this invaluable material so that they may also know how to become and stay rich. Next, use the information to begin the implementation of your own plan to building wealth. Finally when you begin to achieve a level of success you previously never had, be sure to give back in your own unique but meaningful way. One that will have a positive impact on the less fortunate people. I thank you in advance for reading and it is imperative that you take action NOW!

I wish you much success.

Ken Botwe

www.ingramcontent.com/pod-product-compliance
Lightning Source LLC
Chambersburg PA
CBHW052317220526
45472CB00001B/153